YOU CAN MAKE IT!

Library of Congress Control Number: 2019934640

ISBN: 978-1-63308-472-8 (paperback)
       978-1-63308-473-5 (ebook)

Cover and Interior Design by *R'tor John D. Maghuyop*
Cover Image by *Eugène Delacroix*

CHALFANT ECKERT
PUBLISHING

1028 S Bishop Avenue, Dept. 178
Rolla, MO 65401

Printed in United States of America

YOU CAN MAKE IT!

TWELVE KEYS
TO VICTORIOUS FAITH

GARY M. DUKE

CHALFANT ECKERT

PUBLISHING

TABLE OF CONTENTS

DEDICATION

To my amazing wife Gina, who has never stopped being my greatest source of encouragement and support and without whom this book would not have been written.

I love you Sparky!

FOREWORD

I am honored to have been asked to write the Foreword to this book by my very dear friend Gary Duke. I am privileged to have known Gary and his family for many years. During those years, I have witnessed the transformation of a man who having faced many storms triumphed physically, emotionally, and spiritually. Gary is a shining display of God's grace, hope, and restoration. His insight into the heart of a matter will captivate and keep you focused as he instructs his readers through the process of facing potential storms, surviving the onslaught of the storms, and restoring the pieces left scattered by the storms. This book will give you hope that no matter how dark the storm clouds may be there is a silver lining that comes through trusting in God's Word and persevering without wavering. Gary encourages us in this book to always keep our eyes focused on Christ so we can stay on course no matter what while remembering the words of the Apostle Paul:

For which cause we faint not;
but though our outward man perish,
yet the inward man is renewed day by day.
For our light affliction,
which is but for a moment,
worketh for us a far more exceeding
and eternal weight of glory.
While we look not at the the things which are seen,

but at the things which are not seen:
for the things which are seen are temporal;
but the things which are not seen are eternal.
2 Corinthians 4:16-18

I pray that no matter what storm is raging at this moment in your life, you will be enlightened by the instruction God has given Gary through years of facing his own personal storms and breaking through with overcoming victory!

Tina Borden
Co-Pastor, First Assembly of God in Livingston, Texas

INTRODUCTION

If you are reading this book, I hope that you are going through a trial. It is not my desire to wish you ill will. It is my desire that as a result of the labor of love you now hold in your hands that strength, faith, and hope will begin to emerge in ways you have not yet experienced. My prayer is that you, like me, will enjoy the privilege of seeing that trial pass leaving nothing behind but a sense of triumph.

I have experienced a lot of struggles. It was not until recently that I was able to deal with my trials in the manner that God intends. Most of my past trial experiences were accompanied by words of doubt and fear. I did not know that a person could truly face a struggle with an uncertain outcome and experience joy and growth. At least, I had never personally accomplished it until now.

I wrote this book with the thought in mind that perhaps someday one of my children or grandchildren would be in the midst of a great struggle and on the verge of giving up. I considered the possibility that I very well may be dead by then. If so, I would hope that in the middle of their darkest moment, their eyes would fall on a dusty manuscript written by an old preacher. It is my prayer that they would open the cover, turn the pages, and drink in the truths that God allowed me to discover. I would hope that they would pass on these truths to their children and others they love.

Each chapter was inspired by the Holy Spirit. I know this because even I could not believe what flowed from my soul at times. As each chapter was completed, I read it to my wife, Gina. Tears would flow, and my heart would be touched by what I can only describe as God-breathed. I have not discovered anything that others do not already know. I am only reminding those who read this of the truth that has always existed. Sometimes we just need to be reminded.

More than anything, I want you to know the greatest truth of all which is: *YOU CAN MAKE IT* — not in your own strength or by human intervention, not by pop psychology or positive thinking, and not by anything other than the means that God has already provided for us to utilize. I pray that you find the peace that always exists in the eye of the storm and the joy that always comes after it passes.

CHAPTER 1

FAITH IS FUNNY

L ife is funny. Just when you think things are going your way something always happens. Often, it's something that you least expect. Sometimes it involves people you least suspected as well. Sometimes it's tragedy and other times it's a pleasant surprise. No matter what, it usually rocks your boat or causes you to step back and realize that you are a lot more vulnerable than you think.

I started a journey about a year ago. I have been a Christian now for thirty-two years. I have been in various aspects of ministry. I started out preaching evangelistic meetings and a few revivals. I went to Bible college and began pastoring a church. That church turned into another church, and then taught Bible college, and then another twelve years of pastoring. During that time, I became involved in counseling and began working at a *Teen Challenge* unit for about six years. During that period, I went back to school and became a professional counselor. That was thirteen years ago. I also helped plant a small church for about a year. Through it all, I can truly say that life has thrown me several proverbial curveballs.

Spirituality in itself is quite perplexing. We can have the desire to be what we believe God wants us to be and still fail miserably. Part of the failure lies in our misunderstanding of what "good" is. For many years I assumed that God was trying to fix me — and believe me, I was broken!

> SPIRITUALITY IN ITSELF IS QUITE PERPLEXING. WE CAN HAVE THE DESIRE TO BE WHAT WE BELIEVE GOD WANTS US TO BE AND STILL FAIL MISERABLY.

I grew up in the home of a Pentecostal preacher who genuinely lived what he believed, but that didn't seem like much fun to me as a young man. I had an older brother who had discovered all there was to experience in 1968, and that seemed much more appealing to me than going to church three or four times a week. So, I never really gave God a chance. I was the typical preacher's kid who you did not want your child hanging out with unless you thought your child needed his worldview changed. I brought weed to the youth meetings, played guitar in church tripping on LSD, and was one of, if not the main source of illegal drugs in my high school.

By the time I reached adulthood, I was seeking out playmates my brother's age rather than my own and I had become a criminal. Drugs, alcohol, and pornography were the symptoms, but lack of affirmation and insecurity were at the root of my problems. Of course, like most criminals, I got caught. Passing forged prescriptions for narcotics all over the Dallas-Fort Worth Metroplex produced a three-year sentence in the Texas Department of Corrections. Notice it is called the Department of "Corrections," not the Department of "Rehabilitation." So even after my stint in jail, my problems persisted.

On June 14, 1986, all that changed. I was twenty-nine years old and a hopeless heroin addict. I weighed about 130 pounds and looked like death warmed over. I had just got arrested for shoplifting at a Target department store. I was trying to get enough from refunding the item I stole to get one more shot of dope in my veins. The next five days I went through withdrawal in an observation cell, which seemed more like hell than anything else I had ever experienced. My brother convinced my dad to bail me out, and I found myself kneeling at the side of a bed contemplating my life. I realized that I had tried practically everything that the world had to offer, and yet I was still very empty. I prayed a simple prayer that no one led me in. They didn't need to. I merely told God that if He really does "save" a person that I am a perfect candidate. "Please save me." And He did.

> I REALIZED THAT I HAD TRIED PRACTICALLY EVERYTHING THAT THE WORLD HAD TO OFFER, AND YET I WAS STILL VERY EMPTY.

That was the first time in my life that I could truly say that something totally unexpected happened to me. I woke up the next day *wanting* to go to church! That in itself was a huge piece of evidence that the supernatural had occurred because I hated church. That same day was Father's Day. My dad got the best gift he could have received — a prodigal son who once was dead was now alive and had come home. I also received a gift that day.

I was sitting in a church for the first time in years, and God gave me a vision. I was looking at the minister, and suddenly the entire front of the church looked like a big white movie screen. The edges looked like a cloud. It covered everything. Suddenly a book appeared on that screen. It was opened up, and there was nothing on either side of the page. A hand appeared as well with part of an arm covered by a white sleeve. With the index finger, that hand wrote my name, Gary Duke, at the top of that page. It disappeared as quickly as it appeared. I was shocked, amazed, and confused. I never forgot it though, and it has always been a benchmark for me whenever I began to doubt my salvation experience.

Not long after my conversion, I felt that I was called to share the Good News with others as a minister of the Gospel. I met my wife two months later. She was a 24-year-old virgin who had been a Christian since she was eight years old and had already graduated Bible college. She lived on a farm. I could not for the life of me figure out why her dad did not like this newly regenerated ex-con, ex-drug addict from Dallas. He had to learn to love me though because we were married in six months and have been together now for thirty-one years. Like I said, life is funny.

We were blessed with two beautiful daughters who also kept themselves for their husbands and are now living wonderful lives of their own. We have two amazing grandsons and two awesome sons-in-law who both love Jesus and our daughters. We struggled financially for the first twenty years of our marriage, but a master's degree and a counseling career alleviated the pressure somewhat. I was able to build my wife the dream home she drew on a piece of paper years before I even met her. I have a good reputation and have remained clean with no drug or alcohol relapses. It sounds like a success story, and in many ways it is. However, there have been many struggles, failures, and challenges ... or should I say curveballs?

Faith is kind of funny, too. Right when you think you have it down pat, you must actually put into practice what you tell everyone else is so easy. Except it doesn't quite work like that when it's *you* that is being put to the test. My father-in-law used to say, "A man with experience is never subject to a man with a theory." In other words, it doesn't matter what you think you know if you haven't actually put it to the test. Yeah, faith is a lot like that. A person can be experiencing what they believe to be the very presence of God for a good while and then something happens that threatens them, and they are not sure God is anywhere to be found. Suddenly they have to *believe* that He is there. They are forced to *know* what the outcome is before it occurs. They must operate on God's time rather than their own. They have to *trust* that He is going to show up. Yes, *faith* is funny.

> "A MAN WITH EXPERIENCE IS NEVER SUBJECT TO A MAN WITH A THEORY."

We can experience the spiritual life. It is evident. After all, most everyone would agree that we as humans consist of body, soul, and spirit. Even atheists will agree with that notion. We are constantly searching for spirituality in one way or another. I remember during the sixties when for a short time, drugs were seen as the gateway to spirituality. That was, of course, until people started dying. I don't think that was the type of spirituality they were really searching for.

Some people attempt to discover deeper spiritual meaning through self-discipline. Others claim that yoga and meditation are the keys. Still, others look to nature as the source of inner peace. I have always thought it interesting that God seems to be the last choice for the majority of people seeking truth and tranquility.

I remember when I was in Bible college that I read a huge book about world missions. It said there has never been a civilization ever discovered that did not worship some sort of god, even if it was the moon, sun, or even a rock. There is something within every person that bears witness that there must be something or someone beyond ourselves that has a better understanding on this thing we call life — the task of discovering that something or someone is called a spiritual journey.

One thing I have discovered about a spiritual journey is that we will never reach our destination on this earth. If we could, someone would have done it by now. My father-in-law, (I might as well call him by his name since I have already referenced him twice), Henry, loved to travel backroads. When he took a trip of several hundred miles, he generally took the scenic route. He took extra hours to get to his destination because there were yard sales along the way holding treasures he wanted. He would say that it is the journey that he enjoyed, not the destination. This is the crux of a spiritual journey as well. We will eventually reach our destination if we are on the right road. It is up to us what we gain along the way.

> ONE THING I HAVE DISCOVERED ABOUT A SPIRITUAL JOURNEY IS THAT WE WILL NEVER REACH OUR DESTINATION ON THIS EARTH.

I have learned quite a bit on my journey in the last thirty-two years. One of the things I have learned is that I do not have what it takes to make it on my own. I am a weak individual prone to sin and self-gratification. The baggage I brought into my relationship with Christ was overwhelmingly large. I have spent the most of those thirty-two years attempting to unpack it all. I have not completed that task yet. My addictive personality is always lurking in the dark seeking to draw me into its grip like a drug pusher in a dark alley. Some people call it their "demon." I am a child of God. I don't have demons. What I do have is baggage.

I heard someone say once that addiction is like taking your car to the beach. If you ever take your car to the beach, you will never get all the sand out of it. Regardless of how many quarters you push in the slot at the local car wash, there will always be a grain of sand stuck somewhere in the crevasses of your vehicle. Addiction is similar. I have to remain aware and vigilant because there will always be a remnant of addiction tucked away in the wrinkles of my brain. Occasionally a grain becomes dislodged in the form of a drug-using dream or a brief craving. If addiction cannot manifest itself in the old way (shooting up or getting drunk), it will seek new ones that work just as well. Success, materialism, accolades, and lust are just a few of the substitutes it employs.

Another truth I have learned is that being accepted by Christ and pleasing Christ are two entirely different things. Anyone can come to know Jesus. He made it so easy that the young and simple would have the same opportunity as the sophisticated and intellectual. Salvation is a universal call that anyone can understand and respond to. It is the most significant decision you will ever make, and it will determine your eternal destiny. Not everyone agrees, but everyone will bow before the Lord. Christ is the door that every person must enter through to experience eternal life — His words, not mine.

> ANOTHER TRUTH I HAVE LEARNED IS THAT BEING ACCEPTED BY CHRIST AND PLEASING CHRIST ARE TWO ENTIRELY DIFFERENT THINGS.

But to *know* Him is entirely different from merely accepting Him. Meeting a person and knowing a person are two different things. If a millionaire meets me and gives me a million dollars, I can say that I know something about that man, but I cannot say that I truly know him. I may be rich, but I am not clairvoyant. In order to know him, I must develop a relationship and discover what kind of person he really is. That requires me recognizing the character traits he possesses, the focal point of his life, his dreams and goals, and what brings him pleasure. It would also mean that I would discover what he does not like and what offends him. To learn these things takes time and effort. It is a journey of sorts. Even with great investment of time, I would still never know him fully. You and I are made in the image of God, and like God, we can never be fully known by another individual. I am not sure we can even fully know ourselves.

Yet despite the impossibility of reaching the destination on this planet where we reside, we are given the awesome privilege of enjoying the journey! God is willing to feed us information that is eternal in nature if we will but pursue the task of achieving it. He gave us a book called the Bible which is full of more clues and principles than Dan Brown could ever have imagined in his *The Da Vinci Code* (2003, Corgi Books). It is not nearly as obscure either. In fact, spiritual truth is quite obvious if we will open the eyes of our hearts and behold it. Too often we forget our material world can be a distraction to the spiritual truths we desperately need to embrace so that we can become whole. No wonder Paul told the readers in Colossians:

Set your affections on things above,
not on things on the earth.
Colossians 3:2 (KJV)

God wanted us to understand spiritual truths so much that he sent a part of the triune Godhead to Earth. The man we call Jesus who said He was the Son of God, came from heaven and walked among us. He taught us eternal truths so we might better understand how to experience spirituality. He pretty much had to. We would never be able to figure it out otherwise. Satan was already well established in teaching man a whole other side of spirituality which leads to an entirely different destination. It was a brilliant move on God's part and on our behalf to send Jesus to earth. Jesus taught us how to live our lives so that we are pleasing to God. We just have to be like Jesus! How much easier can it get? Right?

Wrong. Actually, we make it much more difficult than it has to be. The problem is that *proclaiming* faith and *exercising* faith are not the same. It is easy to profess to others what we have been told regarding this life of faith. However, when it comes down to where the rubber meets the road, it becomes much more challenging. Suddenly the trouble we are experiencing seems unique to us. We begin to believe that we are the only one who is really being challenged. Everyone else is on the bunny slope, but we have exited the ski lift and found ourselves right in the middle of the Giant Slalom of life. That is when the hypocrisy of what we say and what we do becomes obvious.

> THE PROBLEM IS THAT PROCLAIMING FAITH AND EXERCISING FAITH ARE NOT THE SAME.

Authors more astute, profound, and articulate than me have written books about faith and facing life's challenges. They may have dwelled on a deeper plain of spiritual awareness than I do, but I know for sure that we all experienced challenges that we could not conquer alone. We all tried to fix our problems through our own efforts and found that inadequate. They, like me, probably discovered the end of themselves, and in their desperation and fear, learned the true meaning and value of faith.

That is my story. I wish I could say that after being a Christian for a few months, or even a few years, that I grew so quickly that I was prepared to handle all that hell could throw at me. I would love to relay to you that during the many years I stood behind a pulpit and so confidently told others how to survive the onslaughts of the enemy that I was the epitome of a spiritual conqueror. I wish that I could tell you that I am the poster boy for faith and at the bottom of that poster there is a quote in bold capital letters that says, "NO WEAPON FORMED AGAINST ME SHALL PROSPER!" (Isaiah 54:17). Yeah, I wish that was the case.

Unfortunately, that is not the case. In fact, as I review my walk with Christ, I can say that I have failed many more times than I have been faithful. I have had to ask God to restore my soul more than all the sheep in the Middle East put together. I have thrown up my hands many times in the midst of trials and looked God square in the face and asked the age old question, "Don't you care?"

I have done these things not because I wasn't trying hard enough. It was not the lack of effort that put me in such a lame place with the Lord. It was not because I did not have access to spiritual knowledge. It wasn't that I just needed someone to explain the Bible to me. It wasn't even because I lacked a prayer life. I prayed a lot. I read a lot. I tried hard. The problem was that I did not truly understand faith. I was stuck in the stereotypical concepts that I had been taught and had taught others for so long. I believed with all my heart, I just believed the wrong thing. Or maybe I was just hard-headed.

If so, I was in good company. I look at the twelve men Jesus handpicked and realize that I am just as smart as they were. They weren't any more insightful than me. They laid down their secular jobs and pursued spiritual gain ... so did I. They tried to stay close to Jesus ... so did I. They were willing to be used to advance the Kingdom of God. That's my story too. They were as dumb as a box of rocks. Uh ... yeah, so am I.

I look in the Bible, and I find that the one trait man has consistently exhibited in terms of how to live a life of faith is *a short memory*! Let's take for example Abraham, the first of the Hebrew patriarchs. God spoke to him numerous times and promised him a son. Regardless of how many times God showed up and spoke to Abraham, he still could not remember what he had been told directly by God. You would think that if you heard the voice of God speak to you the same message on several occasions as well as see the fire of God with your own eyes, you would eventually grasp hold of what was being said.

> I LOOK IN THE BIBLE, AND I FIND THAT THE ONE TRAIT MAN HAS CONSISTENTLY EXHIBITED IN TERMS OF HOW TO LIVE A LIFE OF FAITH IS A SHORT MEMORY!

The children of Israel were great examples of short-term memory loss if ever there was one. I mean, come on man! Ten plagues, Red Sea finale, water from a rock, quail dropping out of the sky, bread on the ground every single morning, and so on and so on — yet, still dumb as a box of rocks. I guess even God can't fix stupid.

Then there was Elijah. What a man of faith and power he was. In one day, he called down fire from heaven, stopped a drought, physically outran a chariot for about twenty miles on foot, and personally killed hundreds of false prophets with his bare hands and a sword. This guy was on fire! Yet, in a short time span of a few hours, he was running for his life and hiding in a cave because a wicked queen wanted him dead. He was depressed and suicidal, and God started moving Elijah's ministry over to Elisha.

In the light of these stories, and many more that time does not allow me to relay, I find a certain amount of comfort. They tell me that we are all subject to memory loss when it comes to faith. I can't tell you all the times God has come through for my wife and me. He has performed numerous miracles which could only be explained supernaturally. He has been one hundred percent faithful. He has never failed me or disappointed me or given me a reason to doubt Him. I now find it perplexing as to why it took me thirty-two years to obtain the keys to faith that I had not previously possessed.

I have been through numerous trials in my life. The trial I experienced in this last year was not extraordinary. It was not a battle with cancer or some other life-threatening disease (thank God). It was not a financial strait that would be so devastating that we would be destitute. It was not something that threatened to destroy my family or marriage. It was not what seemed like endless nights of sleeplessness wondering where my wayward child was. It was just a trial.

I have been through many trials in my Christian experience. For the first twenty years of my marriage, we lived pretty much hand to mouth. I pastored a small church and worked as a self-employed overhead door repairman and installer to make ends meet. There were plenty of opportunities when I could have gained the knowledge that

I obtained in this last trial I am about to describe. I should have gained that knowledge. However, for some reason I always went through the current trial in the same fashion I had gone through the one previous. If I had to describe what that looked like using only emotions as adjectives, I would have to say whiney, angry, frustrated, worried, apprehensive, and discontent. That is not an exhaustive list. It's merely all I am willing to admit at the moment. Needless to say, I was not the picture of God's man of faith and power.

> I ALWAYS WENT THROUGH THE CURRENT TRIAL IN THE SAME FASHION I HAD GONE THROUGH THE ONE PREVIOUS.

Yet, all of those trials ended the same way. God would allow them to progress to the point that I realized that without some sort of divine intervention on His part, I was pretty much doomed to whatever level of destruction I could imagine. Then, as always, He would come through in the nick of time. Oh, I would rejoice then! You could hear me singing the praises of my faithful God and how He always takes care of His children. That was not the song I was singing in the midst of the trial. My song during the trial was the ole song they sang on *Hee-Haw* when I was a kid:

> *Gloom, despair, and agony on me*
> *Deep, dark depression, excessive misery*
> *If it weren't for bad luck, I'd have no luck at all*
> *Gloom, despair, and agony on me*
> Buck Owens and Roy Clark, 1969

This time it was different. It was different because it came right in the middle of the greatest spiritual journey that I had possibly ever embarked on. My wife and I left the church we had served for twelve years. For the next several years, we attended at least three different churches before we landed at one where we chose to stay. It wasn't that we were flakey, uncommitted churchgoers; we were just aimless. After twenty years of ministry, it was hard to assimilate into the body as just believers. But the thought of being involved in any capacity was unappealing. We told ourselves that we just needed to sit and soak. We had just given everything we had to offer to a group of people and a community who for the most part seemed unappreciative. I didn't give a lot of thought that Jesus' resume looked very similar.

We finally decided to attend at the church where our daughter, son-in-law, and grandkids attended. It was not the type of church I had been accustomed to, but I had already come to the realization that I was just going to have to settle for what was offered and be happy. The people in the church were friendly enough. I felt free to worship God, and they were teaching the Bible. The pastor was an older gentleman who treated me nice but did not seem to value my wife and me as assets even with all the experience we brought with us. I tried to overlook the negatives and accentuate the positives.

Over time, the negatives seemed to be much more blatant than the positives, and I grew critical. That critical spirit evolved into spiritual dryness. I told myself that I really didn't need church. If it weren't for my daughter, I would just stay home every Sunday. I didn't recognize it, but my soul was slowly slipping away from God's presence. I was also oblivious to how it was affecting the way I viewed myself and others.

I was dying a slow death. The evidence of that spiritual decay was starting to show up in a variety of ways. My language became increasingly more corrupt — not just in terms of the use of slang or even occasional curse words, but also in my hateful opinions that I would often express. Out of the heart, the mouth speaks (Matthew 12:34). My heart was not a good scriptwriter at that time. My addictive personality began to manifest itself, and my perceived emotional needs were not being met by those I expected to come to my rescue. That usually results in some form of self-gratification.

The person that hated me most was me. I was discontent and disgusted with where my spiritual walk had taken me. I tried to read the Bible, but it seemed like there was nothing in that book that I had not already heard. I would pray, but I felt like God wasn't listening because my heart was not genuine. I had been in the ministry long enough to know that there was nothing anyone else was going to tell me that I didn't already know, so I sought no help and no counsel from others. I was in a hopeless situation. I did not think that I could ever regain the type of joy or faith I once had. I wondered at times if I ever really had it to begin with.

But God is so amazing. He saw that I needed help and He reached out to me in my time of need. My other daughter and son-in-law attended a church in Joplin, Missouri. It was a different denomination. We visited on Easter Sunday to spend time with our kids (and as a perfect excuse to miss our own church). The service was well orchestrated, and the message seemed to hit the bullseye in my heart. The Spirit of God touched me. I felt something I had not experienced in a while. When Mother's Day rolled around, I came back. Again, I sensed that God was trying to do something fresh in my heart.

I came one last time without my wife to see my kids before they went on a summer-long ministry trip. It was during that service that I made a commitment to God. I told God, "Okay Lord, if this is the place you want me to be for a while, I will come all summer long and see what happens." I did just that. Every Sunday I drove an hour by myself and sat in the same place five rows from the front on the end of the aisle. It was one of the strangest experiences I had ever had.

Each week, I would show up, and people greeted one another and were friendly, but no one ever spoke to me. It was as though I was invisible! They walked around me, by me, and what seemed like through me. At first, it was kind of disconcerting, as though they just weren't being friendly. I knew that was not the case because I saw how they responded to each other. I became aware that this is exactly how God planned it. He did not want me to become a member of the church or even to build relationships there. This church was the operating room that God chose to perform heart surgery on a preacher lying in spiritual ICU.

Every week I got stronger. God began to revive my joy, and my desire for the Word of God returned. I began to listen to several sermons on CD every day and would soak them up like a sponge. Every service ended with communion. As I would sit there with those elements in my hands, I realized that this entire business was between God and me. No one else was involved or needed to be involved. He was dealing with me directly. I grew more spiritually in those three months than I had during my entire life.

Summer was ending, and I wondered what would be next. My wife also wondered and she missed me sitting beside her every week. She was not about to discourage this growth spurt, but I was certain she was curious about the future. So was I.

We went on a vacation which included me speaking at a friend's church in Texas. That Sunday morning the subject of Sunday school came up in our discussion. I told him that I always loved teaching a class and that I would jump at the chance to do it again if the opportunity arose. Be careful what comes out of your mouth…

We were on our way back from Orange Beach, Alabama and had decided to return a day early. The church I had been attending for the summer was having a day of service in the community, and I had not volunteered because I was not planning to be there. It was literally the end of summer as we define it on the calendar. Gina, my wife, asked me what I was going to do as far as church attendance, and if I would be going to Joplin the next day. I agreed to attend with her the next day instead. It had been three months since I had sat on the seat next to her.

I walked into the church, and within minutes the pastor who had previously seen little value in me approached me. After he greeted me, he immediately asked a question. "There is a need for a class to be taught on the book of Revelation. Would you be willing to teach it?"

I was thinking, "Are you kidding me, God?" I had no intention of ever coming back to this church. The Lord reminded me of the words I just spoke one week prior to my friend, and through almost gritted teeth, I agreed to teach the class.

Approximately four months later, the pastor resigned and another man took his place. The new pastor was loving, kind, and obviously valued people. I started to feel as though something was occurring that I had not expected. I looked at my wife with tears in my eyes one Sunday as we were pulling out of the parking lot and told her that I felt as though God had us there for a reason. It was as if hope had risen in my heart that I could somehow once again be a part of church ministry in some capacity other than senior pastor. I am presently an elder in that church body. Life is funny.

Two months after returning to the church, things got dicey in my life. I am a professional counselor in private practice. Two and half years prior I had begun supervising a lady that was seeking full licensure. She was a great therapist and a delightful person to be around. She had lots of trauma in her past, and I felt that I could make a difference in more ways than one. We became close friends as well as colleagues.

The woman's practice consisted mainly of children's therapy most of which was funded through state Medicaid. She had her own business working for family services before I met her, and had her own office. She maintained her own files and did all her own billing. She never indicated to me that she had questions regarding how to bill or that she was struggling with maintaining documentation. Her practice grew, and in the previous year, she had billed the state over $70,000. However, since she was not fully licensed, all her payments were funneled through my business account. The state paid me and I, in turn, paid her. I took none of the money and was merely a go-between.

One day I received a phone call from the state indicating that they were coming to audit the files. I told the auditor that I would not be there because the files were not mine and I did not do the work. She reminded me that I would be liable for any money that might be recouped. I told her I understood but was confident everything would be in order.

Everything was not in order. As a matter of fact, the state audited sixty-three files, and every one of them contained errors. I was informed that in three months they would notify me how much I owed. At first, my colleague was very remorseful. She indicated that she would pay whatever was owed and that I did not need to concern myself with it. Honestly, the bill could be anywhere between $1 and $70,000. It was a very serious matter. I was extremely disappointed in her and angry that she had placed me in that position. I trusted her, and she had let me down.

Things got worse. Within two or three weeks, this friend and colleague went from remorseful to protective. I received a phone call indicating that she was doubling the rent on my office space and that she wanted me to sign a month-to-month lease. Although she was now fully licensed, she continued to bill for services under my name. I felt like I was in a hole and she was digging it deeper. She also had all my personal information such as pin numbers and passwords. I felt the need to pull back on the reins a bit, so I changed my login info. The day I did that she evicted me from her office building and severed all communication with me. I was now on my own to clean up the mess she had made. My business and family were financially at risk. That was the trial I faced.

In times past I would have totally freaked out. I would have laid awake every night pondering every possible scenario. I would have been so consumed with anger that part of those nights would have been spent plotting my revenge. I would have lost faith and confidence in God and would have wondered why He allowed this to happen to me when I was doing nothing wrong and was experiencing my greatest period of spiritual growth. In times past, I would have been a wreck. I had just paid my taxes for the year and had a few hundred dollars in savings. I had no feasible solution other than to trust God for a miracle.

It was during these four or five months that God taught me more about faith than I could ever hope to learn. It was the first time I had ever gone through a trial *victoriously*! What is victoriously, you might ask? It is the ability to maintain your joy. It is a daily sense of confidence. It is sleeping well every night despite your circumstances. It is learning not to have animosity against the people that caused the trial. It is not feeling like a victim. It is growing stronger in the midst of it rather than feeling drained and beat down. It is all this and much more.

Through this trial, God taught me numerous faith lessons that I will never forget. I recorded them in the "notes" app on my phone. I knew He did not want me to forget them. I also know that He wants me to share them with as many people as possible. That is why I wrote this book.

It is my hope that the next several chapters will change lives. I pray that regardless of what trial a person may face that these truths I share will be a source of strength and insight. I know that my trial may seem petty compared to the one you are going through. I would be the first to agree. But in God's eyes, all trials are petty. I also know that His truth and solutions are not dependent upon the magnitude of our problems but rather the awareness of

> IT IS MY HOPE THAT THE NEXT SEVERAL CHAPTERS WILL CHANGE LIVES. I PRAY THAT REGARDLESS OF WHAT TRIAL A PERSON MAY FACE THAT THESE TRUTHS I SHARE WILL BE A SOURCE OF STRENGTH AND INSIGHT.

the help that is constantly available. People are destroyed by lack of knowledge (Hosea 4:6). I hope that you will be able to gain some knowledge from what I am about to share. I will never view a trial the same way ever again.

The next few pages contain what I believe to be keys to victorious faith. I do not claim to have gained unique insight that no one else has ever gained. Nor do I believe that these keys are all there are to offer. I am still in a learning process, and I am sure that I will come to other truths in the future. For now, these are what I feel that God would have me to share. They may be old hat to some people. For me, they were revelations of truth that changed my life. I pray that they will have the same effect on you.

CHAPTER 2

PATIENCE

*It takes greater faith to wait than it
does to see an immediate answer.*

I was raised in a Pentecostal church. For those of you who have
never attended such a church, some clarification is likely
needed. First and foremost, they believe in the baptism of the
Holy Ghost. I say *ghost* because if you say *spirit*, you obviously
were not raised in a Pentecostal church. Please allow me to give
you a crash course in Pentecostalism 101.

The baptism of the Holy Ghost is an experience separate from
the salvation that a person receives when they are completely
overtaken by God. The proof or evidence of the reality of that
experience is what is known as "speaking in other tongues." This
is when a person yields his or her speech functions to God, and
He speaks through that person in a language that is unknown to
the person speaking. If that sounds really odd, then you were not
raised in a Pentecostal church. If you are accustomed to that type

of church, it is perfectly normal and something that we believe every Christian can and should experience.

One of the benefits of being full of the Holy Ghost is that you become a person that the Spirit can flow through more easily as well as communicate with more clearly. In other words, you become more susceptible to be used in the "gifts" of the Spirit Paul spoke of in 1 Corinthians 12 such as prophecy or healing. Jesus said that the disciples would receive power when they received this gift. Primarily that power is so that one can live a life that is pleasing to God. One of the benefits is also increased faith. This increased level of faith can be utilized in the operation of the gifts of the Spirit when the need arises. So, the more of the Spirit you have, the greater the faith and power you will possess. This is what I was taught for years.

What I learned most recently however is that some of that just isn't true. For example, just because you have been baptized in the Holy Ghost (which I have) and pray in tongues (which I do) does not mean that your faith is more effective than those who have not. As a matter of fact, it might even hinder you because you may be placing your faith in an experience or your own perception of spirituality rather than in God or what He has declared in the Bible.

As a Pentecostal believer and minister, I believed that if I prayed the prayer of faith, it would come to pass. If it does not come to pass, it may be an indication that my faith is too small or perhaps I do not believe wholeheartedly. It could also mean that I have some sin in my life that is blocking this prayer from being answered. Of course, the last option would be that God has chosen to not answer the prayer at that moment for some reason unknown to me. That option is not very attractive because it usually means that I lack faith, doubt God, or have secret sin, and the entire thing goes into a tailspin at that point. After all, Jesus did say that if you ask anything in His name, He would do it (John 14:14). So, if it is not happening, it cannot be because God has a mind of His own and is refusing to be at my beck and call, especially since I am full of the Holy Ghost AND I speak in tongues!

It is difficult to fathom that God sometimes chooses not to answer our prayers. When a person is battling cancer and we pray, we want to see God intervene immediately. The thought that He would delay that healing is foreign to who we believe God is. Why would He not answer the prayer? Does He take pleasure in seeing us suffer? Is there a reason why He shows up so inconsistently? What's the deal? Why does God enjoy jerking our chain like that?

> IT IS DIFFICULT TO FATHOM THAT GOD SOMETIMES CHOOSES NOT TO ANSWER OUR PRAYERS.

I believe the answer lies in several truths. First, God is sovereign. He is the one in charge. While He may choose to grant our request the very moment we ask, He may also choose not to. One reason for what seems like inconsistency on His part is that He is trying to teach us something or help us to grow spiritually.

As I was going through this tough time in my life, I sought to gain as much faith as I could. I began listening to audio sermons numerous times per day. I chose a wide range of speakers, some of which had Pentecostal backgrounds — the strength and boldness of the voices of men like A. A. Allen and RW Shambach cannot help but infuse me with a sense of spiritual unction. I love hearing the stories of miracles that had taken place in their ministries and how God is just as real today as He was in the Old Testament.

I wanted to have the kind of faith that would enable me to speak healing or deliverance into someone's life. I have no doubt God can do it because I had seen miracles in my life as well as in my dad's life. I formed the habit of prayer as my knee-jerk reaction to every problem. This is not a bad habit to form. I prayed believing that if the request was made, it would come to pass. There was no reason to believe it wouldn't. God works like that sometimes. However, sometimes He doesn't. Not because our faith is weak, but rather because He has a bigger plan in mind than we know about.

In the midst of my own trial, my wife had a situation occur. I was sitting in our den watching a baseball game when I happened to look over at her and saw something troubling to me. It was a look. It was not an angry look. It was not the kind of look that made me want to turn the television off and trot off to the bedroom either. It was a look of fear. For some reason, fear had crept into the mind of the person that I love more than anyone on earth.

I asked what was wrong. At first, she said nothing, but then said: "I have a bump on my leg." That was somewhat of a relief because the look she had given me implied more like a lump in her breast than a bump on her leg. I asked to see it, and there it was. It was a very pronounced bump on her shin. It looked more like a lump than a bump, and it was hot with fever. It just looked like she had hit it against something, but there was no bruising.

"Does it hurt?" I asked.

"Very much!" she replied.

"Did you hit it on something?" I inquired further.

"Not that I remember," she said.

Immediately I saw an opportunity for God to use me, His man of faith and power, to speak this knot into utter oblivion. "Well…we will pray that knot off of your leg right now!" I boldly proclaimed. I laid my hand on the affliction and immediately began commanding it to flee in the name of Jesus! I sounded like one of the tent evangelists I had been listening to daily. I took my hand away hoping to see it disappear right before my very eyes. It didn't. I prayed again — same result. Well, even Elijah had to pray a few times before he got the job done, so I made one more attempt. Nope, it was still there.

"Well, it will be gone in the morning" I declared with confidence. It wasn't gone the next morning or the morning after, or the day after that.

In the meantime, I discovered the origin of the fearful look she had given me. We both had done the absolute worst thing a person can do when they have a puzzling affliction: we had Googled it. There it was. It was plain as day. This knot could very well be and in our minds had become a blood clot. The masterminds of Google declared to us that this was a life-threatening situation. Should that blood clot that we diagnosed with Google break into smaller blood clots, my wife could die. Don't judge! I know you have done the same thing at least once.

So now God had placed me in a position to learn a lesson regarding faith. Here we were going through a financial trial with a bill we had no idea how to pay or how much it was going to be, and suddenly we may have a hospital visit. I prayed some more with greater boldness and volume, but the results remained the same.

Finally, feeling defeated and spiritually weak, we made our way to the doctor's office. I was the last one out the door, and I was all alone in the house. I did not want my wife to hear my cry of frustration and confusion. I said in a loud but broken voice, "God, don't you know we don't have the money for this? Why is this happening? Why don't you do something?"

We were sitting in the examining room when the doctor walked in. He took a quick glance down at my wife's leg and said, "Oh, you have a contusion."

We looked at each other and said, "Huh?"

"A contusion," he said. "Does it hurt?"

"Yes, a lot," she replied.

Then he looked straight at us and said, "It's not a blood clot."

It was as if he had dealt with enough foolish people in his career that he knew a couple of "Googlites" when he saw them. We learned that it was nothing more than an internal bruise and that it would go away in time.

My wife's leg was the seed God used to teach me a faith lesson. The next day or so God began to show me the faith key I needed. That key was that great faith is not exemplified by immediate results. As a matter of fact, immediate results have nothing to do with great faith. Immediate results have nothing to do with us but have to do with the timing God chooses.

GREAT FAITH IS NOT EXEMPLIFIED BY IMMEDIATE RESULTS.

28

When Christ came down from the Mount of Transfiguration, He found His disciples attempting to hold a faith healing service. The only problem was that no one was getting healed. A man had brought his afflicted son to them looking for help. The symptoms appeared to be epileptic-type seizures resulting from demonic influence. When these seizures occurred, the boy often attempted to hurt himself. It was a very serious situation. Fortunately, Google did not exist then. The father had heard about Jesus and His disciples and came for help. For some reason, the disciples could not get the job done. They had been successful in the past but failed with this boy (Mark 9:14-29).

When Jesus appeared, He encouraged the father with the thought that all things are possible if he would only believe. Then that dad spoke some of the bravest words ever uttered in the Bible: "Lord, I believe. Help my unbelief."

Wow! Can you imagine being that honest with God? He was willing to admit that there was something lacking in his level of faith that made it incomplete. There was some doubt in his mind that kept him from being "all in."

What happened next should not be astounding to anyone. If we believe that God is a loving, caring Father and that Jesus was the bodily representation of the Father, it should come as no surprise. Jesus healed the boy.

Of course, He did. That's who Christ is. Notice it was not dependent upon the perfect faith of the man nor was it done in the time frame of the disciple's busy schedule. The Lord began to show me that real faith lies in trusting God's timing instead of my own. The disciples asked Jesus later why they had failed.

REAL FAITH LIES IN TRUSTING GOD'S TIMING INSTEAD OF MY OWN.

He told them that sometimes it takes fasting and prayer to see the miracle you seek. I believe what He was really saying was that sometimes you must wait on God.

Fasting and prayer are great works, but they are still just works. It's something we do to achieve something else. It is not the act of going hungry or talking to God that makes the difference. It is the fact that we recognize that our nature does not gel well with God's divine plan at times. We want what we want when we want it. That's who we are. The thought of waiting patiently is usually not that appealing.

Society has become increasingly influential in instilling impatient mindsets within us. Everything must be done as fast as possible, or it is outdated. I can order an item from Amazon one day, and the UPS man delivers it to my door the very next day! That is scary! I am wondering where this guy lives and how he knew how to find me so quickly.

Our computers and cell phones are measured in speeds that I for one do not understand. What is even crazier is that we can somehow discern when they are not doing what they do quite fast enough. "My computer is slow," we say. Really? Slow? Do we even remember what slow looks like? Slow was cutting out x number of box tops and mailing them into some company in New Jersey and waiting four to six weeks to get a cardboard pair of x-ray glasses only to discover that they aren't all they were cracked up to be.

It should not surprise us that God makes us wait. He has always made man wait. God called Abraham to be the father of many nations when Abraham was 75 years old and promised to give him a son from his wife, Sarah, when Abraham was 90 years old. A decade later when Abraham was 100 years old, that son was born. In the meantime, Abraham had to wait. Abraham's faith grew as he waited on God to fulfill the promise. He became more and more acquainted with who God really was and how important it was for him to hold onto the promise he had been given. He also learned that it wasn't okay to try to rush God or take matters in his own hands.

God never gets in a hurry. God doesn't wear a watch.

That theology does not sit well with us. We see no value in Him making us wait. After all, the longer the problem persists, the more discomfort we feel. Anxiety

GOD NEVER GETS IN A HURRY. GOD DOESN'T WEAR A WATCH.

and fear slowly creep in and little by little we begin to doubt whether God is even aware of the issue. We even begin to question our relationship with Him or worse yet, His very existence. In other words, our faith begins to fail.

That is why patience is such an important key to faith. When we are aware that God is not in the least bit concerned with time, our trial becomes much easier to endure. The question is not whether God is going to solve the problem or when He will do it. The question is whether we believe that He will remain true to His Word and what is He trying to accomplish during the process.

I heard Dr. Tony Evans give an illustration once that helped me to understand more fully how God views our problems. He spoke of going to a parade. We have all been to one at least once in our lives. We stand on the sidewalk and patiently wait for the sound of the marching band or the horns and sirens of the local police and firemen. As the parade moves down the street, we strain our necks to see what is coming next. We can often see two or three things at once. Perhaps we see the band marching out of step right in front of us, and behind them, the homemade float prepared by our local bank. Finally, if we lean forward enough, we can even see a couple of the classic cars coming around the corner a block or so down the street. That's about all we can see until it progresses a little further. That is our vantage point.

God, on the other hand, is like the Goodyear Blimp. He sees the entire parade from start to finish. He can easily see all that is involved. He is aware of where it starts and where it ends. He can see how fast it is progressing or if there is a problem with one of the floats holding up the progress. Yes, He sees it all right down to the horses at the end and the guys with the poop shovels keeping the streets clean. He sees it all.

One of the biggest barriers to victorious faith is that we want to orchestrate the results. That is a problem. We are not in charge. God is very creative in how He interacts with us. He is also extremely multifaceted. No one can multitask like God. At any given moment, He is accomplishing a number of things in our lives and using a variety of situations and circumstances to do it.

Faith is really all about trust. God asks us to trust His wisdom and most of all His nature. He wants us to believe that He is in control and that He will remain faithful to His Word in spite of how things look at the moment. That requires patience. We are often asked to wait.

Most of us hate to wait for anything. We are not geared to waiting. Our flesh grates against the idea of being put on hold and listening to music that is not of our choosing until someone other than ourselves decides it's time to move forward in the conversation. I have learned that waiting is an intricate part of God's plan in developing our faith. We have some background information that helps us with this issue if we choose to refer to it.

Take Moses for example. God saved Moses' life and placed him exactly where he wanted him. He was set up like a bowling pin to be the leader of Egypt during a time when Egyptians had control over the Hebrews. Perhaps the storyline would have been much different if Moses had not taken matters into his own hands. One thing we know for sure though is that God put Moses on hold for 40 years in a place we know as "the backside of the desert" (Exodus 3:1). That does not sound to me like a pleasant place to live, but apparently, the Egyptian police rarely ventured that far so it worked for Moses.

When it seemed like his life was doomed to mediocrity and his dream of being a leader of something more than a herd of sheep had died, God showed up. It quickly became apparent that the story wasn't over. In fact, it was just beginning. God's stopwatch reached zero and immediately it was game on! Suddenly all the waiting Moses had done was in the rearview mirror, and there was nothing but windshield time ahead as God moved this guy forward at breakneck speed.

David had to wait as well. Can you imagine the day that he came face to face with the prophet Samuel who was the legend of his time? Just the thought of this great man of God showing up at your house would have been exciting enough. But for a young boy like David to stand in the kitchen in front of his parents and his brothers and get saturated with Wesson oil, and then be proclaimed the next king of Israel would have been overwhelming. No doubt David felt the Spirit of the Lord flow over him as much as he did the oil. But then what?

Wait! That's what. Wait. Go back to doing what you were doing before and wait until God makes a way for the vision to come to pass. That is what David did. He went back to his sheep and waited. He learned a few things while he waited. He learned that God knew who he was and where he was. He learned that God wants worship more than anything else. He learned that being alone with God on a hillside could never be replaced by any palace. He learned that with God all things are possible. He learned that it was going to take more than his own strength to accomplish the job he had been called to do but that God was able to empower him. Finally, he learned how to sling a rock super well.

Even Christ waited. We aren't given all the details, but the wait was obvious. At age twelve, we see Jesus sitting in the temple teaching the teachers. When questioned by his parents, Jesus said that he must be about His Father's work. There is an obvious gap between age twelve and age thirty. What was going on during those eighteen years? Waiting. That was what was going on. Waiting.

Jesus had to wait until it was the right time for Him to reveal Himself. He would not have been accepted as a rabbi or teacher unless he was at least thirty years old which is the age of leadership in Judaism. His entire existence on this earth was planned before the world was ever spoken into existence. Paul wrote that,

When fullness of time was come,
God sent forth His Son...
Galatians 4:4 (KJV)

God had been waiting as well. There were over 400 years of silence before John the Baptist burst on the scene declaring that Jesus was the Lamb that takes away the sins of the world (John 1:29).

I remember reading in a book on world missions that the birth of Christ could not have come at a better time. Rome ruled the world. One of the things Rome was known for was road construction. They built roads everywhere because they wanted access to the places they conquered. The saying "all roads lead to Rome" was a factual statement. Because Rome ruled, there were no borders to stop a person from passing from one territory to another. As a result, the ability for Christian missionaries like Paul and Apollos to reach the world with the Gospel was much easier.

The Greeks had greatly influenced the world as well. Because of the conquests of Alexander the Great, most of the world spoke a common form of the Greek language. People held onto their native languages, but speaking Greek was almost essential to do business and conduct daily affairs. As a result, the ability to preach and teach the Gospel to all people was possible.

God waited to send Jesus into the world so the time would be ripe to receive His message. Jesus waited to reveal Himself so that the greatest impact could be made on those He came to save.

The trial you may be going through has an end in sight. The Bible tells us that many are the afflictions of the righteous, but the Lord delivers us out of them all (Psalm 34:19). The issue is not *if* God is going to bring your trial to an end. The truth I am trying to convey in this chapter is that the issue is not *when* God will bring your trial to an end either. The real issues is whether you will rest in the fact that it *will* end and that there is a purpose in it.

Patience is the ability to endure while maintaining your peace and joy. The alternative is suffering through a trial and experiencing the anxiety that accompanies the uncertainty of the outcome. The Bible says:

> **PATIENCE IS THE ABILITY TO ENDURE WHILE MAINTAINING YOUR PEACE AND JOY.**

> *In your patience possess ye your souls.*
> Luke 21:19 (KJV)

The Greek word for patience (*hypomone*) means cheerful endurance (*Strong's Exhaustive Concordance of the Bible*, 5281, 2009). Thayer defines the word as the characteristic of a man who is not swerved from his deliberate purpose and his loyalty to faith and piety by even the greatest trials and sufferings (Thayer and Smith, *New Testament Greek Lexicon*, 1999).

James declared that the ability to wait or exhibit patience during a trial brings about a state of maturity not otherwise achieved. He indicated that it would help make us "complete" and "lacking nothing."

> *But let patience have her perfect work,*
> *that ye may be perfect and entire, wanting nothing.*
> James 1:4 (KJV)

David tells us in the Psalms how to wait. His instruction to us is based on his understanding of who God is. Knowing God's nature is paramount to victorious faith. David had a relationship with God that went beyond what many others before him had described. The Bible says that David was a man after God's own heart (1 Samuel 13:14 and Acts 13:22). No other chapter in the Bible depicts this more than Psalm 51. After committing adultery and murder, David appeals to God's mercy. This was in the time of the Law. The law clearly stated that the penalty for such sin was death. But David knew God. He knew that God's mercy extended beyond the realms of the law and made his case based on God's nature rather than God's commands. God restored David though not without consequences.

David describes the method of waiting on God in a way that is most beneficial to us and most pleasing to God:

- We should wait without shame – Psalm 25:3 states that going through a trial does not mean that we have willingly placed ourselves in a place of displeasure with God. Our trial is often not a reflection of our standing with God. Satan tried to use my trial to make me ashamed in other's eyes as though I deserved it. I became aware of the role that pride plays is hindering victorious faith.

- We should wait with a teachable spirit – Psalm 25:5 says we should seek to gain the knowledge and insight that only comes from struggle and suffering. As I went through this trial of waiting, I remained sensitive to anything that God wanted to use to reveal new truth that would aid me in the process. The trial itself made me a sponge for knowledge and revelation.

- We should wait with courage – Psalm 27:14 tells us that courage is not ignoring the problem. Courage is the resolve to see it through with confidence that victory is the outcome. When David marched onto the battlefield to fight Goliath, he did so with courage. That courage sprang from an awareness of who was really facing the giant that day. It was not a shepherd boy but a representative of Almighty God who would be doing battle. I kept reminding myself that I am God's child and that He is the One in charge of His property.

- We should wait peacefully – Psalm 37:7 indicates that Satan wants to steal our peace. He delights in keeping us awake at night fretting and worrying. I determined not to allow my emotions to control me. *Emotions are great followers but lousy leaders.* I took thoughts that would create anxiety into captivity by telling myself that I would just not go there. I replaced negative thoughts with thoughts of God's love and power. His Word became my mainstay!

> EMOTIONS ARE GREAT FOLLOWERS BUT LOUSY LEADERS.

- We should wait hopefully – Psalm 39:7 states that the word *hope* as it pertains to God has no room for doubt. I might hope that someone I know would do something nice for me. He or she may or may not. However, *when my hope is in God, the outcome is certain. It is the kind of hope that an expectant mother has when she thinks about the birth of her child. She has no doubt that it will occur,* but her expectancy lies in what the child will look like or how it will feel to finally caress the infant to her breast. My wife and I would talk about how God was going to solve our problem. We did not discuss *whether* He was going to do it, but rather what it may look like or how it will feel *when* He does. I developed a hope or expectancy that actually sustained me, rather than entertaining a haunting fear or doubt.

- We should wait obediently – Psalm 37:34 tells us that oftentimes we are at a loss of what to do during a trial. The answer is to do what is right. In the midst of trouble, there is often an opportunity to take matters in your own hands and act in ways that are contrary to God's plan. We can easily justify our actions by saying we are suffering wrongly. That will hinder faith. There is an assurance that comes with knowing that your actions are above reproach. During this trial, I did some things that I found hard to do in order to maintain my integrity, but I found that in doing so my faith grew mightily.

- We should wait worshipfully – Psalm 52:9 exhorts us to give God praise above all else! The last thing that Satan wants to hear or see is a saint praising God. After all, Lucifer, the old devil, was kicked out of heaven for rebelling against God and he hates us praising God during our trials. One of the best things to do in a trial is to give God thanks. Thank Him for what He has done, is doing, and what He is going to do. I started every day (and still do) with a time of prayer and thanksgiving. It is this ongoing communication with God that helps us maintain the inner joy needed to sustain us. God deserves our praise, and our situation does not change that.

- We should wait with His word – Psalm 130:5 says the greatest faith builder is God's Word. I saturated myself in the Word during the trial I experienced. I started and ended each day with God's Word. I read the Bible, listened to numerous sermons, and listened to Gospel music. Feeding your soul and mind with God's Word is essential if you plan to maintain victorious faith. There is no substitute!

Therefore being justified by faith,
we have peace with God through our Lord Jesus Christ:
By whom also we have access by faith
into this grace wherein we stand,
and rejoice in hope of the glory of God.
And not only so, but we glory in tribulations also:
knowing that tribulation worketh patience;
And patience, experience; and experience, hope:
Romans 5:1-4 (KJV)

BUT WE GLORY IN TRIBULATIONS ALSO:
KNOWING THAT TRIBULATION
WORKETH PATIENCE;

CHAPTER 3

OBEDIENCE

*In the midst of every trial, you will be
required to perform an act of obedience.*

Faith requires action. Action often requires obedience.
Obedience usually involves us doing something that we
would not normally do (or at least something that would
not have been our idea). Take Abraham for instance. Here was a
guy that waited decades for a son. He and his wife conceived in
their old age. It was a miracle by anyone's standards. Sarah was
90 years old at the time of the birth! This was the son that God
declared would be the heir to all that God had promised. Then
God throws Abe a zinger.

God tells Abraham to take his son, the promised son, up on
a mountain and sacrifice him to God like he would a lamb or a
goat. Okay, first, this goes against everything that God is about.
Nowhere in the Bible do we see that God tells anyone to sacrifice a
child to Him. In fact, we see that this practice was an abomination

to God. Secondly, if Abraham sacrificed his son Isaac, who was going to take his place and become the heir? The entire idea was preposterous. Nevertheless, that is what God told him to do. I think that there was not a lot of doubt as to whether God actually said it or not. It must have come in the form of a deep baritone voice right out of the sky.

What we see next is amazing. Genesis 22:3 states that Abraham rose up *early* the next morning and made his way to the place that God had directed him to do the deed. He took his son and bound him hand and foot. He laid him on an altar of wood that he had prepared. He took out a knife that he had no doubt used many times specifically for the purpose of cutting an animal's throat. Abraham was about to take Isaac's life when he heard that same voice once more.

> *And he said, Lay not thine hand upon the lad,*
> *neither do thou any thing unto him:*
> *for now I know that thou fearest God,*
> *seeing thou hast not withheld thy son,*
> *thine only son from me.*
> Genesis 22:12 (KJV)

It was all a test. Isaac was never in danger. The all-knowing, omniscient God who knew exactly what He was going to do and how it was all going to turn out asked a man who was already faithful to prove it by being obedient to a command that made little or no sense. What kind of madness was that?

The end result was that Abraham would always be able to look out his window at that mountain peak and be reminded that God was everything that he knew Him to be. It would reinforce for the rest of Abraham's life that God had indeed chosen Isaac to be the heir to all that God had promised. It would be a constant reminder that God is faithful to provide. For in that last minute, God also had prepared a ram to take the place of Isaac on the altar. Finally, Abraham would always be aware of the blessing of obedience. It was because of his willingness to obey that he was privileged to live out this incredible experience.

Obedience is a key to victorious faith. Throughout the course of a trial, there will be things you must do to exercise your faith. Faith is not a state of mind — it is a committed heart (exhibited by what we do) based on what we already know about God. Dr. Tony Evans puts it this way:

> **OBEDIENCE IS A KEY TO VICTORIOUS FAITH. THROUGHOUT THE COURSE OF A TRIAL, THERE WILL BE THINGS YOU MUST DO TO EXERCISE YOUR FAITH.**

Faith is acting like it is so even when it is not so,
in order that it might be so, simply because God said so.

He knows the plans. Follow Him every step of the process. Throughout the course of my most recent trial, I reminded myself of this little saying almost daily.

Not long after my colleague severed all ties with me, something interesting took place. I received a check in the mail. It was for work she had performed. The amount of the check exceeded $1,000. So here I was waiting to receive a bill from the State of Missouri which could easily be in the tens of thousands of dollars. It was a debt that I had played no role in creating. The person who caused this problem had evicted me from my office costing me a couple more thousand as well. I had no reason to believe that she would take any responsibility for any of the money that would be owed. But here I stood holding a check for $1,000.

Under favorable circumstances, every penny would have gone to her immediately. This was not favorable circumstances. I immediately saw the check as a down payment on the huge sum of money I would soon be expected to pay. "At least I will get a thousand out of her," I thought. The money had been direct deposited, and I made a mental note to treat it like a *GoFundMe®* account. Finally, it appeared that there was a little divine retribution taking place. In my opinion, it was overdue. She deserved all the pain God wanted to dish out. I felt somewhat vindicated.

However, over the next week or so, those feelings of revenge begin to fade. I began to sense that God was speaking to my heart something that I did not want to hear. I could hardly believe what the Lord was telling me. I prayed every day hoping it was my imagination, but it was not. I could not escape the fact that God was directing me to send her the money she was owed. The bottom line was that she had done the work and the money did not belong to me. Although she was costing me an untold amount of money and had placed me and my business in an uncertain situation, God still wanted me to do what was right.

I argued with God. "But God…" I said, "You know I don't have the money to pay this bill, and she was the one who caused all this!"

None of that seemed to concern the Almighty. What did seem to be on His to-do list was for me to exercise faith and obedience. It was essential if my faith was to be perfected.

I recall the day I made the decision to submit to God's will in this matter. I was working out on an elliptical machine at my local YMCA, and God began to appeal to my heart. He reminded me of the many times He had shown up in bad situations throughout my life. He assured me that He had not changed. He also reinforced the thought that in His way of looking at things, obedience on my part was a primary issue. Slowly my heart began to melt inside my chest. I knew that despite how my flesh felt, I had to do what was good and right. I sent the check.

I did not lose a thousand dollars that day. I gained a little more faith and confidence in God. There is a sense of confidence that comes from being obedient in the face of difficulty. I love the song "Blessed Assurance" written by Fannie Crosby. These lines give great comfort:

Blessed assurance, all is at rest,
I in my Savior are happy and blessed.

We must partner with God if we expect Him to work miracles on our behalf. God does not partner with those who are disobedient or underhanded. If I had kept the money, God would not have overlooked it, and the still small voice would have gotten louder, and my peace would shattered because of my disobedience. Ultimately, God had always been CEO of my agency, and He was making an executive decision. I could choose to obey and be rewarded, or I could face the consequences. The moment we begin to take matters into our own

WE MUST PARTNER WITH GOD IF WE EXPECT HIM TO WORK MIRACLES ON OUR BEHALF.

hands He steps away. We can't be in charge. We must determine who is going to run the show.

The decision is sort of a no brainer. God has all the resources needed to solve any problem. He is the only One who can change circumstances that are out of our control. He knows the ins and outs of all the elements involved. He also is the only One who knows the entire plan that is being implemented. We can only see one step at a time, but God knows the beginning from the end. If we choose to disobey His orders, we do so to our own demise. However, when we form the habit of acting in obedience to His promptings, we open the door to the supernatural. We form a partnership with God. He is not afraid to show us what He is capable of if we will just be willing servants and let Him have the reins. The best way for me to explain this is to give you some personal examples that have taken place in my own life.

The first church I served as pastor was located in what I like to call the "armpit" of Missouri. It was a small town on the outskirts of Carthage Missouri. I will not mention the name because there are still people who have the misfortune of living there. Let it suffice to say that it was a very humbling place to serve God. The population was less than 300, and every house had a broken-down vehicle in the front yard. A police officer told me once that it was originally a place for thieves and robbers to hide. He said they are still there; they just grew too old to steal any longer.

I was attending Bible college, and my wife was teaching first and second grade at a Christian school about thirty miles away. We ran an eighty-mile paper route daily to supplement the fifty dollars per week we received for being pastors. Our oldest daughter was three years old, and we had just had our youngest. Yes, times were lean.

The church we served was off the beaten path. We rarely had a visitor show up for a church service. The congregation was made up of a couple of families that had been there for many years. This congregation had made most people in town mad more than once, making evangelism nearly impossible. The residents liked me but hated the church. We were pretty much stuck financially. Things were not going to get much better.

Typically, the first Sunday of every month was "Missions Sunday" in our denomination. It was a day that pastors all over the country urged their parishioners to give a little extra to support those who were trying to reach the heathen in foreign lands. Our church was no different. Funding missionaries was not on the top of the list with these folks. When we arrived to begin our time there, they were supporting one missionary family (former pastors of the church) to the tune of five dollars per month. This was embarrassing, even for this church. It was a small congregation, but most were farmers and had the means to give if they had the heart to do so. They did not.

That bothered me. I began to talk to God about how I could get these stingy people to give. He had a different take on it altogether.

"You give," He said.

"Me?" I thought.

Man, if there had been a contest for the person in church least equipped to give more money, we would have won hands down. We were living in an outdated single-wide trailer house in the middle of a cow pasture and barely making it. But God prompted me to give my first-week's salary of fifty dollars each month to missions.

I agreed under one condition. I had to have it to give. I told the Lord that if I had the money in my bank account in the first week of the month, I would be obedient. I was not going to write God a hot check. What occurred over the next year or so built my faith immensely. My obedience opened the door for God to show His ability to meet needs in our lives.

I recall one of those "first Sundays" when we were literally down to the weekly check we were to receive that day. I knew we had the money to give, but I also knew it was all we had. We had a whole week staring us in the face. How would we buy gas for the thirty-mile trip to school and back each day as well as for the paper route? How would we buy diapers? Did we have enough food for the week? These were the questions I had racing through my mind as I obediently wrote that check; I experienced some anxiety in the process.

We returned that Sunday night for the evening service. If we had twenty people attend on Sunday morning, we were lucky to see eight or ten return on Sunday night. This service was no different. As the service ended and the people left, we made our way to the car my dad had given us a year or so before. We always locked the car doors because the neighbors across the street from the church were most definitely carryovers from the robber days the cop told me about.

I unlocked my door and hit the button that unlocked my wife's door. The dome light came on. And there it was! On top of my dashboard,

ON TOP OF MY DASHBOARD, SPREAD OUT IN WHAT I CAN ONLY DESCRIBE AS FIVE FINGERS ON A HAND WERE FIVE TEN-DOLLAR BILLS. MY WIFE AND I STARED AT IT IN DISBELIEF.

spread out in what I can only describe as five fingers on a hand were five ten-dollar bills. My wife and I stared at it in disbelief.

"Didn't I just unlock my door?" I asked.

"Yes," she replied.

"Wasn't your door locked as well?" I asked again.

"Yes," she affirmed.

"How in the world did that money get on our dashboard," I asked.

"An angel must have put it there," she said with tears in her eyes.

There was no other explanation, and we have not found one since. God had rewarded our obedience and was building our faith.

A similar incident happened a few months later in which I again gave our last cent and wondered how we would make it. There was no money on the dashboard that evening. We came home and were having a snack when my dad called from Texas. He informed us that prior to the service at his church, a Hispanic man felt that he should go to all the Sunday school classes and take up an offering for us. He felt that we might need it. In all, he had collected over seven hundred dollars and a piece of Jolly Rancher candy a small child had contributed. I kept that candy for years in my desk to remind me that the blessings of the Lord are sweet.

Years later we served another church as pastors. It too lacked in missionary support, and that became a priority for us to address.

The church was made up of less than forty people, and I worked for myself installing overhead doors to supplement our meager salary. Because of the faith that God had built in my heart from the previous experience, we were able to give as much as five hundred dollars as every "Missions Sunday" rolled around. Our giving built the faith of others in the church. Our church eventually supported over thirty missionaries at twenty-five dollars per month!

We stayed at that church for twelve years. God was faithful for twelve years. We were never delinquent on a bill. We never lacked anything we needed. God blessed us with everything we needed and more. Most of all, God showed us that obedience to His commands builds the faith needed to face the difficulties of life which so often appear out of nowhere.

In the early days of my marriage, I was working for A. B. Dick Company selling copy machines. My sales calls often took me off the beaten path. One day I was traveling through a small central Texas town by the name of Mart, Texas. I got a strange feeling each time I passed through that town. It was as if the Lord was prompting me to try to reach the town for Christ. I did not know anyone who lived there and had never even stopped there to buy a cold drink, but the feeling was undeniable. God wanted me to do something to reach this town with the Gospel.

As was often the case, I ignored the feeling for a while and then told my wife about it. My wife was always supportive of my ministry. But she didn't seem that thrilled to hear about this latest revelation. We were living in a one-room house, and she was eight months pregnant with our first daughter. It was August in Texas. If you don't know how hot hell is, come to central Texas in August, and you will likely do some serious soul searching.

My idea was to hold a five-night series of services that we call a revival. Of course, for it to be a true revival someone needs to actually get revived. I'm not sure this event qualified. I was not acquainted with any of the local pastors. It did not appear that anyone I spoke with in Mart shared my passion or vision.

Of course, the first job was to determine where the services would be held. After some research, I learned of a community building which was being used to feed senior citizens lunch daily. I was told that for ten dollars a night I could use it. The offer came with one requirement. Everything had to be put back exactly as we found it each night. The building had no less than a hundred chairs and probably twenty or so heavy eight-foot tables which had to be taken down and put back up. In addition, we could not leave our sound equipment or musical instruments overnight. Those had to be brought back and forth. Finally, the building did not have air conditioning, or at least they were not open to us running up the electric bill.

Each night my wife and I arrived early and did the work of moving all the furniture in the sweltering heat. But hey, it would all be worth it when the town shows up to find Jesus! Right? Wrong. Nobody showed up. Well, I can't say no one showed up. We had some friends and family who saw our efforts, had pity on us, and a few attended every night just for the sake of encouragement. But not one person from the town attended. It was extremely discouraging.

For the Wednesday night service, the only attendees were my wife and my parents. My dad had been in the ministry for over fifty years at that time, so he was empathetic. I can still remember the message I preached that night. I had felt led to minister about Christ's blood being shed on the cross for our sins. It was obviously a message geared towards a call to salvation. When it came to the end of the sermon, I was weeping over the lost souls Jesus died for and gave a strong appeal for the lost to come to Christ. It seemed really ridiculous since the three people sitting in front of me had all been Christians much longer than I had! I wish I could tell you that townspeople suddenly streamed through the door and a great night of conversion was had. That is not what happened. We loaded up just like the previous nights that we had been there.

In those days, revivals were known to extend beyond their scheduled meetings if a "move of God" was being experienced. I looked at my wife on the way over to Mart on the last night and very seriously said, "I am pretty sure we will be closing out tonight" as if it there was any doubt.

My sweet pregnant wife looked at me and said, "That's good because you will be going it alone next week otherwise." She was smiling, sort of.

The last night was no different than the previous four. A handful of friends came out to support me. I was, as we say in Texas, "lower than a mole." I had been so sure that God had prompted me to do this. I kept thinking that a miracle would occur, or the crowd would begin to grow. I tried not to show my discouragement; however, I am sure it was obvious.

Then something totally unexpected happened. A young man about fifteen or sixteen years old rode up on a bicycle and stood in the doorway.

I came over to him to greet him, but before I could get a word out, he spoke.

"They heard you," he said.

"What?" I asked.

"They heard ya," he said again.

"What are you talking about?" I asked. "Nobody even came," I said.

"They all heard you," He said again.

He then explained that every night just before service would begin all the people in the area came outside and sat in their front yards and on their porches in lawn chairs. We had all the windows open because of the heat and had borrowed a good sound system. He assured me one more time as he was leaving that "they ALL heard you."

Obedience is not about results. Only heaven knows what was accomplished in that series of church services. I can tell you that I have thought of that experience many times during the last thirty years. I have also relayed that story to others who were discouraged in trying to accomplish the work of God and not seeing the results they expected.

When we have the assurance of knowing that we are doing the right thing, it doesn't matter what the results are. God is bound by His word to uphold the righteous. He told us that He is mindful of those who fear Him. Fear is not terror. Fear is a healthy respect and honor that causes us to obey just because God deserves our obedience. It was the first test we read about in the Bible. It was also the first failure.

God placed Adam and Eve in the Garden of Eden and told them there was only one requirement.

> FEAR IS NOT TERROR. FEAR IS A HEALTHY RESPECT AND HONOR THAT CAUSES US TO OBEY JUST BECAUSE GOD DESERVES OUR OBEDIENCE.

Don't eat from *that* tree. Why did He do that? He made man out of dust and Eve out of Adam's rib. He literally knew what they were made of. Why wouldn't He just program them to always do what's good and right? Why did He have to put them to the test? We could still be living in paradise!

God did that because He wanted men and women to show that they loved and honored Him enough to obey. God wanted them to recognize that He had their best interests in mind and that through obedience they could learn that God loved them and would bless them for their good choices.

Obedience is often the key to the result we are seeking. When Jesus performed His first miracle in Cana, He commanded the servants to fill up the large pitchers with water and then commanded then to pour them out. The water became wine. Before the five thousand could be miraculously fed, the disciples had to divvy up five loaves and a few fish between the twelve of them. They then were told to make their way toward the multitude of hungry mouths with little more than crumbs in their hands. In their act of obedience, the crumbs became a feast with leftovers to spare. Before the dead man named Lazarus could hobble out of the tomb in his grave clothes, someone had to roll away the stone. That fact is often overlooked. However, can you imagine the faith it took to do so knowing the stench and feelings of hopelessness that was behind it? Before one blind man received his sight, the Lord told him to go and wash in the pool of Siloam. Would he have experienced the miracle if he had disobeyed? I doubt it.

There is nothing wrong with asking God to take care of our problems; He tells us to ask and to seek and to knock. How often do we take time amid our trouble to inquire what we should do? God shows up in supernatural ways at times. Primarily God uses people. That's us. He uses us to accomplish His will. We are His hands and feet and mouth. He employs our abilities and resources. He requires our willingness and obedience.

God delights in allowing us to be part of the miracle. We do not thwart God's ability or divine plan overall when we refuse to obey. Whatever He sets His mind to will be accomplished in one way or another. However, our disobedience hinders what He wants to do in us. We miss out on the blessing of participating in the miracle and growing our own faith in the process. We also may never know what could have occurred had we just obeyed.

I mentioned that for several years we delivered the local newspaper in order to make ends meet. The *Neosho Daily* is an afternoon paper, but on Sundays, we delivered it in the morning. As I was driving around town at 3 a.m., I noticed a man who worked for *The Joplin Globe* distributing his papers as well. I sensed the Lord urging me to share the Gospel with this guy. This was a prompting that I easily shrugged off.

I had plenty of reasons to be disobedient. I had never met this man. I did not know his name. He was just as busy as I was and probably had no desire to stop in the middle of his run in the middle of the night and talk to some guy he had never met about Jesus! It was not difficult for me to blow it off. Nevertheless, I continued to feel a burden for this man's soul each time I saw him. This went on for two or three weeks.

One day I was talking to a friend who lived in a small trailer park. He began to tell me about his next-door neighbor who had taken his life with a gunshot to the head. I learned that his neighbor worked for *The Joplin Globe* as a delivery man. It was the same guy. God chose me to be a source of hope and help to a desperate individual, but I was too busy to respond to the call. A soul possibly went into eternity without Christ, and I was partly to blame.

I know that I was not the only Christian God had at His disposal. I also know that ultimately the man chose to do what he did. I also know that even if I had stopped and talked to him, the outcome might have been no different. I also know that I disobeyed God.

My act of disobedience will always be a question mark in my life. What if I had been obedient? The story might have had a different ending. Only heaven knows the difference I could have made. What I do know is that I failed. That is how important it is to be obedient. I am thankful that God does not condemn us for our mistakes, but He does expect us to learn from them.

GOD DOES NOT CONDEMN US FOR OUR MISTAKES, BUT HE DOES EXPECT US TO LEARN FROM THEM.

Here are a few things to remember about being obedient to God:

1. God already knows how things are going to turn out — Our obedience is not the determining factor in the outcome as much as it is part of the process.

2. God never asks us to do something that does not require faith — Faith is how we respond to God. It is the means by which He is pleased with our actions.

3. God rarely asks us to do things that make sense — It is the absurdity of the request that gives us the opportunity to show that we trust His knowledge and sovereignty over our own understanding.

4. God is more concerned with our character than He is with our comfort — What we are asked to do will usually stretch our resources, time, or strength.

> GOD IS MORE CONCERNED WITH OUR CHARACTER THAN HE IS WITH OUR COMFORT

5. God never asks us to do anything we are not able to accomplish — He will enable us to do His will if we will take the first step of faith.

CHAPTER 4

HOLINESS

*It is impossible to exhibit confidence in God
with a sin problem present in our lives.*

oliness. The word itself is enough to scare the hell out of us! Or actually, it isn't. That's the problem. It isn't. It is a word that is misconceived and often misunderstood. It is used by some to promote self-righteousness. It is used by others to excuse all that we as human beings are capable of as far as offending God is concerned. In other words, it's one of those words even Christians tend to shy away from if possible.

I recall a period in my life when *holiness* referred to a lot of stuff. It was reflective of where I went, how I dressed, and what activities I was or was not involved in. It even had a bearing on certain home furnishings such as whether I had a television. All these material things were somehow intricately weaved together to produce a litmus test for holiness. Holiness was also regulated by the group I belonged to. There was an ongoing comparison amongst its members so that everyone knew exactly where they stood in regard to the level of holiness they were professing.

I can remember lying in my bed at night extremely anxious because I might become one of the unfortunates in the *Left Behind* 16-book series (Jenkins and LaHaye, 1995 – 2007). I was doing all the right stuff. I just wasn't sure if that was adequate. I knew who I was down deep in my heart and the thoughts that I often struggled with. I was afraid that when the rubber met the road at rapture time that my level of holiness was not going to cut the mustard.

Fortunately, God gave us His word. I discovered a passage of Scripture which liberated me from my doubt and fear in regard to this whole "left behind" thing.

> *But if the Spirit of him that raised up*
> *Jesus from the dead dwell in you,*
> *he that raised up Christ from*
> *the dead shall also quicken your mortal*
> *bodies by his Spirit that dwelleth in you.*
> Romans 8:11 (KJV)

I realized that the golden ticket I needed to make it to heaven had absolutely nothing to do with me. It had everything to do with whether I had allowed the Spirit of Christ to enter and dwell inside of me. Whew! What a relief that was. Later I found out that what we were calling holiness was really legalism.

> THE GOLDEN TICKET I NEEDED TO MAKE IT TO HEAVEN HAD ABSOLUTELY NOTHING TO DO WITH ME.

Then there's the other side of the spectrum. This is where we as Christians realize that holiness only comes through what Christ did on the cross. Our righteousness is as filthy rags (Isaiah 64:6). We couldn't be holy if we tried, so why try? After all, any efforts on our part to live lives that we might consider holy are futile. We don't have it in us. Since it's impossible to do so, why would we frustrate ourselves by endeavoring to even give it a shot?

This type of theology causes holiness to take on a new meaning altogether. It is not anything external. It is all internal. Holiness is a state of spiritual awareness that in God's eyes we are holy regardless of what we do because Christ lives within us and we have chosen to claim His holiness as our own.

That brand of holiness sounds good! It fits well in our lives. It requires much less than the first one I described. It does not seek to oppose the flesh which is oppositional to this whole concept to begin with. In fact, the flesh gets along quite well with this type of theology. It feels good. There's only one small problem, it's wrong. That's not holiness either.

So, what is holiness and what does that have to do with faith? Holiness is twofold. It begins when we come to know the Lord as our Savior. If we could be holy on our own, Christ would not have died on a cross. Jesus' righteousness becomes our righteousness when we accept the price He paid for us. That means that we could not pay for our sins. The debt was more than we could ever pay. He, in turn, became the price needed to pay for us to be in right standing with God.

> JESUS' RIGHTEOUSNESS BECOMES OUR RIGHTEOUSNESS WHEN WE ACCEPT THE PRICE HE PAID FOR US.

When we place our trust that He died in our place, and that He did it for us, and we accept the free gift He offers, we become holy.

The word *holy* means "set apart for God's use" (Ancient Hebrew Lexicon, vituralbookword.com publishing, Jeff Benner). It is the same word that the words *saint* and *sanctified* are derived from. Something cannot make itself holy. It must be declared holy by God. God is the only One who determines whether something or someone is holy. He is like quality control concerning holiness. We have several examples of God exercising His QC authority in the Bible.

The first thing that God declares holy is a day. That's right, a day — a twenty-four hour period of time. In Genesis 2:3, the Bible says that God blessed the seventh day and sanctified it. God declared the seventh day to be set apart for the use of honoring God. It was not to be like the other six days. It was God's day.

Later when Moses was employed to lead the Hebrews out of Egypt, God went on a sanctifying spree! He declared the firstborn among them to be set apart for Himself. He declared that the various animals that were sacrificed to be sanctified. He sanctified the men who offered the sacrifices and even the various tools and instruments they used to do so. It became pretty obvious holiness was a prerequisite if God was going to use something or somebody for anything at all.

Later, in the book of Daniel, we see how serious God is about this whole business of sanctification. In Daniel chapter seven the king of Babylon was having a party. As with many parties, it went too long, and people drank too much. That does not usually end well. People get drunk and act stupid. This party was no exception.

King Belshazzar decided that it would be a great idea to go and get the various articles of gold that they had stolen from the temple in Israel which had been declared holy by God. They drank wine from them. He suggested toasting their false gods and humiliating the true God who apparently had been too weak to save the Jews from captivity.

That was when God Himself decided to crash the party. Or at least part of Him crashed the party. His hand to be exact. His hand appeared, and He wrote the next morning headline before the paper ever hit the press:

> *Thou art weighed in the balances,*
> *and art found wanting.*
> *Thy kingdom is divided, and given*
> *to the Medes and Persians.*
> Daniel 5:27-28 (KJV)

That is exactly what occurred. Belshazzar died that night and Babylon was no longer under the rule of a Babylonian king — all because God did not appreciate someone messing with what He called holy.

The Bible says that prior to us becoming Christians we are seen as "dead in our trespasses and sins" (Ephesians 2:1). That verse also says that when we come to know Christ that He makes us alive or *quickens* us. When you cut your fingernail to the place where there is life, it is said that you cut it to the "quick."

The word *death* in the Bible refers to separation. Death is not final. It is merely a separation of the body from the spirit. To be spiritually dead means that we are living our lives separated from

God. Of course, God is always there. We just aren't connected to Him. If a person dies and goes to hell, it is said that they will experience eternal death or eternal separation from God. In contrast, eternal life is us being in the presence of God forever. Being accepted and alive in Christ is one form of holiness. God can't have anything to do with something that isn't holy. It doesn't stop there. We must pursue a level of personal holiness.

Once Christ enters our lives, God has some fair expectations about how we conduct ourselves. We don't live our lives in ways that produces holiness. However, we should live our lives in ways that reflect it. James 2:20 says, "Faith without works is dead." He was not trying to say that works produce faith or that our works somehow impress God. He was saying that if we have faith that is alive, it will be obvious in the choices we make. We will behave as if we are holy and have been set apart for God's service. We will be good representatives of Christ.

> WE DON'T LIVE OUR LIVES IN WAYS THAT PRODUCES HOLINESS. HOWEVER, WE SHOULD LIVE OUR LIVES IN WAYS THAT REFLECT IT.

Personal holiness is our consistent effort to slam the door in the face of sin when it makes a house call. Sin separates us from God. Don't quote me on that. Quote God. He told Adam and Eve that the day they eat of the fruit of the tree of knowledge that they would die. They didn't drop physically dead. They dropped spiritually dead. They immediately lost their place of fellowship with God as well as

> PERSONAL HOLINESS IS OUR CONSISTENT EFFORT TO SLAM THE DOOR IN THE FACE OF SIN WHEN IT MAKES A HOUSE CALL.

their confidence in who God had made them to be. Prior to sin, they were loved and adored by God. They had communication with Him and recognized His favor on their lives.

All that changed after they sinned. They were afraid. Fear had replaced their sense of confidence and acceptance. They no longer looked to God to meet their needs. They decided they would have to fix the problem themselves. They sewed fig leaves together to cover their nakedness. Sin had rocked their world, and all they had left was their own intellect and ability to solve the problem. The solution fell horribly short.

Sin destroys our faith. When I speak of the need for holiness in reference to faith, I am referring to our awareness of what we are allowing through the back door of our lives. What is it that is residing within us that should be evicted if we are going to feel confident in God meeting our needs? Do we even recognize the power sin has in hindering our ability to fully believe that God is able and willing to solve our problems? It is the greatest tool the devil has in his arsenal. It creates doubt and discouragement.

Let's get one thing clear. We as human beings are never going to be flawless until we arrive in heaven. However, we are required to strive for perfection while here on earth. That would seem to create a dichotomy of sorts that could lead to frustration and misunderstanding. How can we try to be perfect if perfection is impossible to achieve? Seeking perfection is an ongoing process and is based on where we are in our spiritual walk.

When my first daughter was born, the doctor told us that she was perfect. Of course, I knew that already. It was evidenced by the buttons that popped off my shirt because my chest was so puffed out. However, the doctor was referring to her current stage of growth and the expectations on that day. She had ten fingers and toes. Her eyes responded to light. She had no visible abnormalities. She was crying, eating, and pooping. She was perfect!

If she had remained in that same state for the next several years, we would have had problems. As time progressed, we expected her to learn how to walk, talk, and feed herself. She would eventually learn how to go to the bathroom in a much less expensive manner given the cost of diapers. She would need to live up to the expectations associated with her level of maturity.

That's what God expects of us. We are to progress in our abilities as we grow in the Lord. With progression comes responsibility. We are responsible for what we allow to attach to our lives as we gain more and more knowledge. As our relationship with God

> WITH PROGRESSION COMES RESPONSIBILITY.

deepens, we learn that there are some things that hinder the level of intimacy we have with Him. He loves us the same, but we are not as close if we are offending Him.

If we don't walk closely with Him, it becomes a roadblock to our faith when God needs to act on our behalf. It does not mean that He will not respond to our cry for help. It does mean that we have the awareness we aren't making right choices. It also means that Satan has a tool he can use to remind us of how unworthy we are for God to respond. The result is that our confidence in God is lessened based on our awareness of our hidden or unresolved sin.

I have lived with hidden or unresolved sin in my life. I know what it is like to struggle with the fact that I am willingly allowing something to occur or dwell inside of me that I know God hates. For me, that thing was pornography.

Pornography use was the biggest stronghold in my life. I had managed to bury practically every other addiction in my life in the graveyard of God's grace. Drugs, alcohol, sexual promiscuity, foul language, and tobacco use had all been laid to rest within weeks of coming to Christ. But I allowed one zombie to continue to hang around. He just wouldn't die.

It was not a daily struggle. It was not something that I patronized or made excuses for. It was not an issue that I justified or excused by telling myself that no one is perfect. I knew it was sin and that it was not okay. For the most part, I was diligent in addressing the issue. It was more an occasional visitor that I allowed in the backdoor of my life to visit for a while. I would immediately acknowledge its destructive power and feel guilt and shame. I would fall on my face and ask for forgiveness and then expel the zombie for a while, but he always seemed to make his way back.

Occasionally, I would find myself in a difficult situation. A trial would emerge during the same period that I was falling prey to this lingering addiction. When that occurred, my faith was almost nonexistent. I knew the nature of God. I knew that God was a God of mercy and grace. I knew that He had always been there for me in the past. I could not, however, escape the fact that I was not living

> SIN STOOD IN THE WAY OF THE PEACE AND CONFIDENCE I SHOULD HAVE BEEN ABLE TO ENJOY WHEN I NEEDED IT MOST.

up to the state of perfection expected of me. I was a pastor and had been a Christian for many years. I knew better. Sin stood in the way of the peace and confidence I should have been able to enjoy when I needed it most.

Thankfully I was able to put that zombie in the grave for good. It no longer has a place in my life. I can now reach down a little deeper inside of myself and grab hold of the anchor of faith that steadies my ship in the worst of storms. It did not change God's love for me or His willingness to help me. It changed the way I viewed my situation as well as the outcome.

It is impossible to discuss this subject without evoking the idea that our works somehow determine God's view of us. Remember that our standing with God is based on nothing but the blood of Jesus. At no time during my struggle did I believe or consider myself unsaved. That was not the problem. Nor did I ever doubt God's goodness. I viewed God in the same way I always had. He is my loving heavenly Father who only wants His best for me and will never reject me despite my weakness. He loves me despite my faults. My picture of God never changed.

My view of myself did change. Once the sin problem was dealt with, I had a different feeling about myself. I no longer looked in the mirror and was reminded of the deception that was harbored in my heart. I no longer had to drop my eyes when a message on sexual sin was preached because I knew that I needed help more than most in the room. I no longer had to listen to the lies of the enemy who used my weakness and failures as a weapon against me when I called on God to intervene on my behalf. I no longer felt less than perfect. In fact, I felt perfect!

Did I just say perfect? Did that sound like the most prideful misguided statement you likely ever heard? Can a Christian be perfect on this planet Earth? The answer is yes! God wants us to feel perfect. He would not have told us to be perfect if the commandment was impossible to obey. He not only wants us to be perfect, He expects it. Anything less is disappointing to Him. The best part is that it isn't even that hard to do. I'll even let you in on the secret of how you can achieve this state of perfection for three easy payments of $39.99! Just kidding, it's free. It really is free. It is not hard to do because we do not actually do anything. Well, very little anyway.

I struggled for many years trying to be better. A lady told me once that I must be on a slow learning curve because I came to the truth I am about to share only after decades of futile effort. The secret lies in in Galatians 2:20 (KJV):

> *I am crucified with Christ: nevertheless I live;*
> *yet not I, but Christ liveth in me:*
> *and the life which I now live in the flesh I live*
> *by the faith of the Son of God,*
> *who loved me, and gave himself for me.*

A man who spent most of his early life endeavoring to live up to the expectations of those around him wrote this verse. He had managed to achieve a lot. He was well respected as a rule keeper and was extremely involved in his church. He was energetic about promoting his religion and had pretty much devoted his life to protecting it from corruption. His name was Saul (who we later known as Paul).

One day Saul's life came crashing down around him as he became aware that his efforts were not achieving the desired result in

God's eyes. In fact, he was a failure. Thankfully he came to know the truth. He learned that the only way to please God was by allowing Christ to live through him. Saul could not do enough to make himself better. There is no "better" in God's world. God doesn't make anything or anyone better. He just makes all things new.

Here's the secret to dealing with your sin problem. Allow Christ to live His life each day through you rather than you trying to live that life yourself. If we had the ability to live as God expects, Christ would never have come to earth. It was our utter inability and futility that moved God the Father's heart to send His Son Jesus to us so that He could pay the debt we couldn't pay. Jesus made a way for the Holy Spirit to live His life through us every day.

ALLOW CHRIST TO LIVE HIS LIFE EACH DAY THROUGH YOU RATHER THAN YOU TRYING TO LIVE THAT LIFE YOURSELF.

Jesus said that God is a spirit. The only way a spirit can manifest itself is through a human being's life. If a person is demon possessed, it is obvious in the way that person acts. He or she spews vile words and exhibit behaviors that are unnatural. The opposite of that occurs when we allow the Holy Spirit to live His life through us. Suddenly, we are behaving in ways that are unnatural. The things we would normally do in regard to sinful behaviors and thoughts are replaced by those that please God. It also becomes obvious when we do something that is uncharacteristic of God's standard of perfection. Immediately we are aware that the Holy Spirit was not in control. We only need to hand the reins back to Him. The result is that as much as can be expected by God, we live on this earth and in this flesh in a state of perfection.

I love the story of David and Goliath. An entire army was shaking in their boots before one really big guy. And I do mean *really* big. I have never seen a nine-foot giant personally, but I can imagine that Goliath was intimidating. The challenge was simple. One guy needed to volunteer to fight the giant and winner take all. Surely there would have been someone who had the courage or lack of brains to give it a try. But out of an entire army of Jewish fighters, no one felt froggy, so no one leaped into this Battle Royale.

The part of the story I like best is when David shows up and hears the taunts of the big bully speaking ill of the Almighty God. He immediately reacts. "Who does this uncircumcised Philistine think he is talking to?" David asks. You know the story. David walks out on the battlefield and drops Goliath like a sack of potatoes with one smooth stone and a slingshot. Of course, Goliath was not the only one that died that day. Once the other "warriors" saw Goliath fall, they began to pursue the enemy as well.

Here's the takeaway. First of all, David knew who was really being challenged. Goliath wasn't facing Israel. He was facing God. Secondly, David knew that God was his bodyguard. David had already received notice that God had a plan for his life that did not include being defeated by Goliath. He knew God had a purpose for his life. Thirdly, David knew what God was capable of. David had seen God work in the past in the form of taking down a bear and a lion. He knew the power that was at his disposal. Finally, and most importantly, David knew he was not the guy in the fight. God was the One who was on the firing line. David was just the representative.

We can march into any battle with the same confidence that David did. David was just a man. He had flaws and limitations. Some of those flaws resurfaced later in his life. He also knew who he was in God's eyes and what God was capable of doing. He had spent many nights on a hillside alone with God. He allowed God to be his guide. He knew God was his best friend and bodyguard. As a result, there was no fear or hesitation when the opportunity for victory presented itself. Defeat was not an option. God never loses.

Perhaps you are remembering all the times you have tried to put your zombie in the grave once and for all with no results. Maybe you have given up on trying. It is possible that you have bought into the lie that Satan often tells that says that others may find deliverance but you never will. He constantly promotes the lie that you must learn to live with your sin. He even reminds us that God is a merciful God and that His grace will cover our constant failure. Satan is good at taking life-giving truth and twisting it into something that keeps us gasping for air.

> SATAN IS GOOD AT TAKING LIFE-GIVING TRUTH AND TWISTING IT INTO SOMETHING THAT KEEPS US GASPING FOR AIR.

We can live in a state of perfection. We can be at peace with God. We can overcome even the most ingrained and deeply-rooted sin problem. It all starts with the subject of the next chapter, humility. The greatest surge of help comes when we reach our lowest point of self-sufficiency. Some call it surrendering our will. Others describe it as relinquishing control. For me, it was all about finally giving up.

> I AM POWERLESS TO LIVE A LIFE THAT PRODUCES HOLINESS. ONLY GOD CAN DO THAT.

I had to recognize that all my best, well-meaning efforts were never going to be successful. I am powerless to live a life that produces holiness. Only God can do that.

The result of that realization was life-changing not only in my day-to-day decisions but also in the increase of my level of faith. As I allow the Holy Spirit to be the doorkeeper of my life, I remain in a state of readiness for the problems I face. He is like a Secret Service agent that is constantly on guard to shield me from harm and show me the way. I can turn to Him at any moment of the day and expect help and support. He guides my thoughts, my words, and my deeds. I now feel like God is leading the way, He is at my side, and He has my back all at the same time!

The Holy Spirit makes me immediately aware of any decisions I make that are contrary to His will. My heart is open to His gentle rebuke and correction, and I am quick to respond. The result is perfect peace and extreme confidence. My first reaction to trouble is to look to my heavenly bodyguard and take His cue. He is always there. There are no doubts in my mind about whether I can face the next challenge because He keeps me in shape spiritually. If I face the infamous warped wall, I know that He is going to give me a hand up. My faith is based on Him, not on me. Doubt has no place to reside any longer because I am no longer involved in the fight.

CHAPTER 5

HUMILITY

*We must acknowledge that we are powerless
and be willing to receive help.*

I remember hearing a story about a guide in an art museum. The climax of the tour was a breathtaking picture painted by one of the masters of art. The reaction was the same from each group of patrons. There would be gasps of amazement followed by a very appreciative round of applause. Slowly, almost unknowingly, the guide began inching closer and closer to the painting as it was revealed. One day the crowd did not react at all. There was no gasp of excitement or round of applause. The guide was surprised. "What went wrong?" he thought. It was then he discovered he was standing in front of the painting. The beauty of the scene and the work of the master was no longer evident. All that could be seen was the guide.

That is what pride does to faith. It destroys the ability of others to see the work of the Master. It places us in the picture rather than

God. To be quite plain about it, we are nothing without Him. There is nothing within us to cheer about. Many people receive lots of accolades because of their various talents and abilities. We herald them as magnificent and astounding and give them meaningless awards at large galas. Have you ever wondered what those people actually do with all those little statues and plaques? Perhaps they end up gathering dust on a shelf just like my "Closest to the Hole" trophy that I proudly display in my man cave.

If God had a list of all the things He hates, I believe that pride would be at the very top. It stands in opposition to everything God is trying to accomplish in our lives. The word pride appears forty-six times in the Bible. In every passage, bad stuff is associated with it. Apparently, nothing good comes from pride. My favorite commentary of the subject is found in Psalm 1:1 in which David says, "Blessed is the man who sits not in the seat of the scornful." Isn't that what pride does? It puts us in a place where we are quick to point out the faults of others and easily overlook our own.

NOTHING GOOD COMES FROM PRIDE.

Pride has its roots in insecurity. It is pride that causes us to focus on self rather than God. It is the means by which we make ourselves believe that we are somehow self-sufficient and not in need of God's help. Pride will convince us to remain quiet even when we are at the end of our rope. It literally cuts us off from the resources that are available to help us through our times of need.

Pride comes in the form of a lie. That lie tells us that our self-image is more important than reality. How we see ourselves becomes paramount in the desperate situations we find ourselves in. We had rather appear as though we have it all together and in control than to ask for help or receive it when it is offered. Pride is like a looking glass that always shows us a distorted image each time we peer into it.

"Mirror, mirror on the wall, who's the strongest of them all?" we chant.

"You are," pride says, "You don't need anyone, and if you say you do you must be weak!" it implies.

Pride destroys faith. God chooses to use people in everything He does. I heard a message recently by Robert Morris in which he had a conversation with God about this very subject. As Morris enjoyed the Alaskan scenic view from the deck of **PRIDE DESTROYS FAITH.** a cruise ship, he extolled the magnificence of God and how that God does not need anything. The response He got back from God was surprising. "I need you," God said. An argument ensued, but of course, God won. Robert Morris began searching the Scriptures and found not one place where God did not employ man in His divine work after creation. God chooses to need us. God loves partnering with us. He doesn't have to; He just does it. When we allow pride to have its way, we destroy the partnership God gives us the opportunity to share in. While God loves to involve us in the process, all the glory goes to Him. That glory derives from the awareness that we are totally dependent on God. Pride kills that glory that belongs to God. It is impossible to focus on self and God at the same time. One must take precedence over the other.

The first time that pride hindered my faith occurred not long after I became a Christian. I was curious about the experience often referred to in Pentecostal ranks as the baptism of the

Holy Ghost with the evidence of speaking in tongues. I had many people including my wife tell me that this was something I needed. I was told it would give me deeper insight into the Scriptures, more power to live a Christ-like life, and a greater anointing in ministry.

I had felt called to preach not long after my conversion. I began to pursue it right away. I was given several opportunities to preach and each time I was sorely disappointed. I felt like a failure after each meeting. I knew that something was missing. I would have quit except for the burning desire that had been placed within me to share the Gospel. That desire just would not go away. But I stunk at it! How could I fulfill this task if I'm not any good at it?

My wife kept urging me to seek to receive baptism in the Holy Spirit.

"If you would just get baptized in the Holy Ghost, you would see a big difference," she told me. I had already tried that once before and had become discouraged. I would pray and ask God to fill me but to no avail. I was also not about to allow myself to do anything that would make me look foolish in front of any congregation. I was not going to be a spectacle.

If you have ever been to a Charismatic or Pentecostal church, you are aware that doing foolish things is kind of a prerequisite. Or at least it seems that way. I was determined that was not going to be my story. I refused to be seen as one of those out-of-control Holy Rollers!

Once I began making an effort to be filled, I made sure I slowly and inconspicuously slipped down between a couple of pews towards the back of the church, looked around to make sure no one was watching, and then said, "Hit me, God." If you're wondering if that is how you receive the baptism of the Holy Spirit, the answer is no.

As the desire and hunger to preach with God's anointing grew in my heart, my pride began to slowly give way to humility. I found myself more and more willing to admit my insufficiency and need for God. I realized that my flesh was weak and that I was ill-equipped to do the will of the Lord without His divine assistance. My struggle resembled a carpenter who had been given the task of building a house and supplied all the lumber to do so but was given no tools. I knew the job I had been given. I held the Word of God in my hands which I recognized as the material needed to see it come to pass. However, I was powerless without the tool most needed to accomplish the work. That tool was the power of the Holy Spirit. I know there are many men who preach much greater than I who have never experienced the baptism of the Holy Spirit with the evidence of speaking in tongues. I can only suggest that if they did experience it, they would be even more effective than they are right now.

As I came to the end of myself, I realized the role that humility played in this process. I needed only what God had to offer, and it was crazy to think that I could somehow substitute only what He could provide. My breakthrough came when I got so desperate that I was willing to stop eating until He blessed me. I told my wife that God was either going to fill me or kill me! I never missed a meal. I received the baptism the very next morning. I wasn't waiting on God; He was waiting on me. He was waiting for me to become totally dependent on Him and deny my flesh the throne it had been residing on.

Faith plus flesh equals flesh. The flesh is full of pride. God hates pride. God wants us to be totally dependent upon Him. That is why He allows situations to come about in which we have no choice but to trust Him. That is when He shows us that He is all we need. Without faith, it is impossible to please God (Hebrews 11:6). With pride, it is impossible to have faith.

FAITH PLUS FLESH EQUALS FLESH.

The opposite of pride is humility. Humility starts when self-sufficiency ends. It is when we acknowledge that we are not self-sufficient. It is an awareness that we are not so important that others do not matter. It is seeing ourselves in a proper light, through Jesus, the light of the world. It is a willingness to defer to others without fear of losing our position. It is acknowledging that it is someone else's job to recognize us and not ours. It is a lack of fear to appear needy or wanting help. Humility stands against self-promotion.

Humility does not come naturally. There are some people who are humbler than others, but even they had to learn humility. It is not a gift that God gives us. It is a discipline that must be developed. That is why we are commanded to practice humility. We practice something to become better at it. Most of us are lousy at humility to begin with. Thankfully, God gives us the option to humble ourselves or allow Him to do it for us. The former is usually the best way to go.

Humility opens the door for great things to occur. The Bible tells a story in 2 Kings chapter five about a great man named Naaman. This guy was well respected and favored by a king. He was a leader of men and had notoriety and position. But he had a problem. Naaman was a leper. He had an incurable disease that would eventually destroy him. Enter God! God had placed a young maid from Israel in Naaman's household. The maid told Naaman's wife about a prophet named Elisha who could likely heal Naaman's disease. Problem solved, right? Wrong. Naaman was on his way to discovering the role that pride and humility play when it comes to receiving a miracle.

After a stop or two Naaman ended up on the front porch of Elisha, but he was met by Elisha's servant instead. The servant told him to go wash in the muddy Jordan River seven times, and he would receive his miracle. How easy can this get? First, he hears about the miracle worker and then receives a simple command that he is easily capable of fulfilling. He had come prepared to pay almost any amount of money and attempt practically any great task in order to find relief.

Naaman had a problem greater than leprosy. The problem was his pride. He was furious. First, why was he greeted by a lowly servant instead of the great man of God himself? After all, didn't Elisha know who he was dealing with? Secondly, the Jordan River is a nasty mud hole compared to many of the rivers in his neck of the woods. What would an important man like Naaman look like dunking himself like a duck in a dirty old river seven times in front of all his men? What if nothing happened? Then what? He would be humiliated and degraded for the rest of his life. The story would be told over and over how the great Naaman took a mud bath in front of his entire company because some impoverished servant told him he would be healed of leprosy if he did.

Naaman was just about to head home when one of his men spoke wisdom into his ears. This man must have loved Naaman and wanted more than anything to see him receive his healing.

"What if the servant had told you to do some great thing?" he said to Naaman. "Wouldn't you have done it?" he asked. Of course, he would have. It would have been an honor to help God out in that fashion. Naaman would not have objected at all if Elisha had commanded him to climb Mount Mariah or swim across Lake Gennesaret. Naaman could have shared in the glory because of what he had done to get the blessing, but that's not how God works.

God does not want us to help Him out. God does not need our help at all. He wants us to be broken and contrite and humble. He wants us to be willing to lower ourselves not so that we can look bad, but so that He alone can exalt us. God wants us to experience Him without anything present to dilute the glory and power and majesty of who He is. When it is all said and done, and we stand back in awe and say without any doubt whatsoever that what occurred was one hundred percent God, our faith gets strong, and God gets praise.

> GOD WANTS US TO EXPERIENCE HIM WITHOUT ANYTHING PRESENT TO DILUTE THE GLORY AND POWER AND MAJESTY OF WHO HE IS.

Naaman humbled himself. Can you picture this great military leader slowly disrobing before perhaps a hundred men or more? The effects of the disease would have been on display for all to see. He was vulnerable. Every man standing there or sitting on their horses probably thought to themselves how fortunate they were that this was not their plight. It would have been hard to watch as this proud leader, a man among men, had to become like a lowly servant. They looked on as Naaman slowly made his way out into the shallow muddy stream. He likely had to lower himself to his knees in order to accomplish the task of completely submerging himself. As he did, his body sank into the gushy mud underneath him and the debris stuck to his hands as they emerged from the water.

Then it began. You likely could have heard a pin drop. However, if you listened closely, you could have heard the men quietly counting under their breath as Naaman began the painful process of baptizing himself in that filthy water. Each time he came up the inspection was made. He and the men looked for any signs of improvement, but there were none. I'm sure that Naaman thought of walking out of that river after a few dunks. Maybe he even started to get up, and that same man that spoke wisdom to him once before gave him a word of encouragement to keep going.

With each dip, Naaman's pride melted away, and his awareness of how that he was hopeless without a miracle became more and more obvious. There was nothing in the quality of the water that was going to wash Naaman's leprosy away. It would be God and God alone if it occurred. Naaman was no longer in the picture. The work of the Master would soon be all that would be seen.

When Naaman came up the seventh time, the Bible says that his skin was like a baby's skin! The shouts could have likely been heard for a mile. Naaman's voice would have been distinguishable above all the rest. The words he spoke would have had nothing to do with who he was or even who Elisha was. The praise would have all been directed to God. Suddenly the humility turned to joy! That is what James says in the Bible. If we will humble ourselves, God will exalt us (James 4:10). God is not opposed to us being promoted or lifted up so long as He is the One doing it. It is when we promote ourselves that He becomes unhappy.

I love what happens next. Naaman returns to Elisha's house to not only show gratitude but to share what he learned in the process. Naaman professes with all his heart that there is no God in all the earth except in Israel. That is how humility works. It allows us to see God for who He is. Our vision is clear because it is not skewed by our own self-image. We can't see God and ourselves at the same time. Through humility, we can see ourselves as God sees us.

In the midst of a trial, God will often place us in a position where we must humble ourselves. It is a means of teaching us to be like Christ. Christ came to earth in the form of a servant and humbled Himself even to the point of dying on a cross in order that the work of God might be accomplished. Humility was a key feature in the crucifixion. Jesus could have chosen not to die but instead decided that He would put His flesh on the cross so that God's plan could be realized.

> IN THE MIDST OF A TRIAL, GOD WILL OFTEN PLACE US IN A POSITION WHERE WE MUST HUMBLE OURSELVES.

I had a great teacher in Bible college named Gene Canter. Brother Canter was a man of wisdom, knowledge, and humility. His love for his students as well as God was evident every day. He was also a pastor. I remember he told a story about how he and his church members were transforming an old barn into a church house. Times were lean, and the work was being done mostly with donations and volunteer labor.

Most usually there is a process in which construction work is accomplished. A person would not normally put up all the drywall before the roof is secure. However, the volunteers showed up to hang the sheetrock a few days before the roofers. As fate would have it, a torrential thunderstorm showed up a day before the roofers as well. Brother Canter received a phone call from a very disheartened church member who reported that all the drywall had been ruined and had fallen off the ceiling. The damage was even greater than that because the sheetrock had also landed on the piano and organ which was being stored there. To put it mildly, it was a huge mess.

Brother Canter said that he drove out to the property to assess the situation. He too was very discouraged. They had put all they could into the project. Replacing all that had been lost seemed out of the question. Not wanting his church members to see his emotional pain he said he slipped off to a quiet spot away from the others to pray.

"God, I don't understand," he prayed. "Can't you see that I am trying to build you a church?" he asked in desperation.

It was then that he heard God reply, "Can't you see that I am trying to use this church to build you?"

It is humbling when we discover that God's agenda is not always the same as ours. The end result may produce the product we are also attempting to produce, but God will likely have accomplished much more than what we expected. What He accomplishes is more important in the light of eternity than what we expected to accomplish. We are constantly in the process of being formed in the image of Christ. Pride keeps us from yielding to God's perfect will. We tend to believe we know more

PRIDE KEEPS US FROM YIELDING TO GOD'S PERFECT WILL.

than God. We tend to want to do things our way. We tend to want to control not only the outcome but also the process.

The Great Passion Play amphitheater in Eureka Springs, Arkansas has hosted over 7.8 million people who came to witness *The Greatest Story Ever Told*, the outdoor drama of the passion of Christ. On the property, there are other displays. One such display is that of a potter forming clay vessels as they were made in ancient times.

Interestingly, the person who made the vessel was the same man who played Christ in the play. I watched his presentation and listened to him give basic information about the mechanics of the potter's wheel and the nature of the clay. He used his foot to get the wheel moving at a very quick pace. He took the lump of clay and placed it on the wheel. As the clay spun at a high rate of speed, the potter attempted to gently place his hands on the clay. Something very unexpected took place. Suddenly his hands appeared to shake and move violently. It was as if the potter had grabbed hold of a piece of machinery that ought not to be touched.

"Do you know why my hands are shaking so badly?" he asked the crowd. "It is because the clay is not in the middle of the wheel." The potter slowed the wheel to a stop and repositioned the clay in the center of the wheel. This time his hands moved effortlessly over the clay. The clay responded to even the slightest touch of the potter's hands allowing the master craftsman to do with the clay as he wished.

Are you getting the picture? Pride says that we can position ourselves. As a result, God faces nothing but resistance when He attempts to form us into the vessel He has in His mind. Our lack of humility prevents the level of submission needed to become God's workmanship. Only God knows the design and plans to be fulfilled. Pride seeks to usurp authority. Humility empowers God to rule without any restraints.

When I first came to know Christ, He showed me something. I was praying one day, and suddenly I began to see an image in my mind of a lump of clay in two hands. The clay was as hard as a rock. The hands worked diligently trying to work the clay but to no avail. Suddenly a steady drip of water began to strike the clay. Slowly the clay became pliable. The water slowly turned to blood and the scene enlarged. I realized that I was standing at the foot of the cross and Christ's blood was dripping on me. The message was clear. God can make me into what He wants me to become so long as I spend my life at the foot of the cross. If I go it alone, I will become hard and useless.

GOD CAN MAKE ME INTO WHAT HE WANTS ME TO BECOME SO LONG AS I SPEND MY LIFE AT THE FOOT OF THE CROSS.

Faith may consist of humility more than anything else. Jesus told His disciples on one occasion that they could do nothing without Him. Every great man and woman of faith in the Bible had to become totally dependent on God and trust in Him only. Most of the time the situation or circumstance demanded just that. Isn't that when we need faith the most? When it seems that there is no way out, the problem is too big, or the situation is hopeless is when we seek to muster up the faith to overcome. We realize that our best efforts will not even begin to make a difference. It is then that we truly understand the connection that humility has with faith.

In the sermon Jesus gave on the side of the mountain in Matthew chapter five, the *first* thing He said was, "Blessed are the poor in spirit for theirs is the kingdom of heaven." Poor in spirit. In other words, happy are those who are aware of their own bankrupt state because it is then they realize how needy they are. God takes no pleasure in us feeling desperate. He absolutely loves showing us how He can fix the most awful problems imaginable. He merely wants us to look to Him. We need only to take note of the examples given in the Word to prove this fact.

A case in point would be the woman who had suffered from a blood hemorrhage for over twelve years. She was financially busted because she had tried all the natural means available to find a cure but had come up empty. Due to the nature of her disease, she was ceremonially unclean and by law was required to avoid bodily contact with others. She was so weak from loss of blood that she could not even walk. She crawled on her hands and knees through the legs and feet of a crowd in order to touch the hem of Christ's garment. She was not disappointed. Her humility and her faith joined together to produce a miracle.

In another case, a non-Jewish woman begged for Christ to free her daughter from demonic possession. Jesus pointed out to her that as a Gentile she had no right to make such a request. He did so to show those around Him what real faith looked like. She took the rebuke in stride and humbly asked that she at least be treated as good as a dog and be allowed to partake of the scraps that fall from the table of the children of God. She was not disappointed. Christ not only granted the request but also recognized the level of faith she exhibited because of the humility it took to exercise it.

The Bible is full of other examples but the take away is that humility opens the door for God to walk through. Pride stands in the threshold blocking His way. It is okay to feel helpless. There is nothing wrong with needing help. There is no shame in receiving it either. This too is a byproduct of humility because often pride rejects the means that God chooses to help us. As Robert Morris discovered, God chooses to use people in all that He does. Our problems give opportunities for others to be utilized in ways that builds them up spiritually.

I am a giver. I love to give. I truly believe that if God blessed me with a million dollars, I would give most of it away. Many people struggle with the ability to give. I do not. It comes very naturally to me. I have a lot of faults, but greed and stinginess are not on the list. I know that there are many like me in the church. Thank God for us, too! Givers take up the slack for all the tightwads that attend church right along with me. If this was a text message, I would have added LOL at the end of the last sentence.

Givers are not fault-free. I have learned that though I love to give, I also find it difficult to receive. It does not take humility for me to give because I get quite a bit of enjoyment from it. I give because I want to be a blessing, but I would be lying if I said I didn't enjoy the response I get from the recipient or the knowledge of them knowing that I care about them. There is without a doubt a certain amount of pride attached to giving even though we would love to pretend there isn't. Let's talk real life. There is little humility in giving if what you give is available and you like the person that you're giving to.

Humility comes into view when you must sacrifice to give to someone who you don't particularly feel close to, or when you need help and someone gives to you. We all want to feel independent and self-contained. We want to appear to have it all together. All of that is challenged when we are in dire straits. It is hard enough to admit things are bad without having to accept help from others. Have you ever stopped to consider that our need may be part of their story as well? Perhaps God is trying to build their faith by showing them it is better to give than to receive. Maybe they have been seeking the Lord for a way to feel useful in the Kingdom, and your desperate situation is just what the doctor ordered to give them the opportunity to be a key player. Yeah, it is not all about us. That's another fact that emerges from the state of humility.

During my last trial I described earlier, God used two couples to help us in a very tangible way. One couple was a dear pastor and his wife who felt compelled to bless us financially. That was humbling because we had been friends for many years. I wept as I received the check in my hand and expressed gratitude to them for their concern. I also felt that their offering was like a seed that was planted in my heart that God did indeed care. It seemed like a confirmation that He was in the process of solving the problem.

The second couple was my daughter and her husband. That was humbling. It was done in a way that they hoped would remain anonymous, but I am a good detective. I figured out quickly that they were the benefactors. I can't describe exactly how it feels for your youngest "baby" daughter and her husband to sacrifice to help pay a bill with my name on it. Her husband had not been a devoted believer for a long a period of time. He was my son-in-law for goodness sake. Any man will tell you that the last thing you want is to appear weak or needy in the eyes of the man that married your daughter.

They did not do it just once either. Twice during this process, they availed themselves to us, and much of the burden was lifted off my shoulders. My pride was pushed down, and humility rose to the occasion. I could not have accepted it except for the effect I saw it had on them as they gave. The smiles on their faces told me that God was blessing them more than He was blessing me. I knew the desire of their hearts. I knew the character they possessed. I knew the love they have for God and their family. I also knew they were taking full advantage of the opportunity to be a blessing to not only their family member but a fellow child of God.

If I had allowed pride to overrule humility, they would have been cheated out of what they received by being obedient. As a result, they grew closer to the Lord, and in turn, their faith was strengthened. Nehemiah 8:10 says that the joy of the Lord is our strength. They stored up some joy because of their willingness to be obedient children of God. That joy would come in handy because within a couple of months they were facing their own trial of a different sort. That's kind of how it works. We build each other up because all of us are in the process of becoming that vessel on the wheel.

How is pride hindering your faith? Who is God willing to use to bless you, but you are not willing to receive because of pride? Have you slowly inched closer and closer to the painting so that you are totally blocking the view of the Master's design?

The solution lies in getting a fresh view of ourselves in the light of God's holiness. In Isaiah chapter six the prophet received a vision of God which made him look at himself in a different fashion. That's right; I said prophet. He was a person who was already well established as a man of God and being used every day in the palace of a king as a spiritual guide. One day he caught a glimpse of who God was. The vision of God's throne was like letting the sunshine in a room that is rarely used. All the dust became visible. There had been spiritual neglect. Perhaps Isaiah had become a little proud of himself and had come to trust in his position and reputation a bit too much. He cried out, "Woe is me! I am unclean." As a result, he sought a fresh cleansing and was suddenly compelled to volunteer for the next assignment God was willing to hand out.

**Humility is not seeing us in a negative light.
It is seeing us in God's light.**

CHAPTER 6

PERSPECTIVE

*The only future Satan knows is what
is written in the Bible.*

One of my favorite authors is Andy Andrews. A *New York Times* bestselling author, he has written over 20 self-help books that sold millions of copies, and is a sought-after speaker. His background is a real-life story of someone who went from living under a pier on the coast of Alabama to being a world-renowned writer. His books connect with the struggles that most people face in every walk of life. One of the characters he made famous was an old man called "The Noticer." The name derives from the character's uncanny ability to help others see things from a different perspective.

In one story a farmer was on the verge of bankruptcy and had gambled his entire future on one last cash crop. Unfortunately, his fields were invaded by hordes of Starlings that devastated his crops as well as his dreams. In a fit of rage the farmer drives his pickup truck into the field, grabs his 12 gauge shotgun and begins blasting as many birds as possible. There were thousands of them. The effort was futile. It was merely a reaction to the hopelessness of his desperate situation. Enter The Noticer.

The old man who has a knack of appearing out of nowhere at seemingly the most inopportune times begins to calmly explore the situation with the bitter and out-of-control farmer. He tells the farmer how fortunate he is to be in this awful situation. I considered that to be pretty gutsy because the guy just lost everything he owned, had nothing to lose, and was holding a loaded shotgun. Then The Noticer begins to explain himself. "Do you realize how many people would like to be in your shoes?" he asks. Astounded at such an insane question, the farmer likely contemplates taking the old man's life as well as his own. But then The Noticer helps the farmer to realize that he is in a position few people find themselves in. He can start over. His life is now a clean slate. He can have a redo. The sky is the limit. The farmer is no longer bound by the constraints of his previous life. He is actually getting a second chance.

In counseling, we call this *reframing*. It is when you take a certain set of circumstances and choose to look at them from a different perspective. In many ways, the beauty of a painting is enhanced or diminished by the frame. The painting is the same, but the frame makes all the difference as to how it is viewed. A Google search for picture frames reveals that there are numerous things to be considered when framing a picture. The frame provides borders for the picture itself. The frame accentuates various aspects of the portrait. The frame adds or detracts from the décor of the room it adorns. The frame should match the size of the painting. All of this applies to how we view the various trials we face.

Too often we choose to make things much worse than they really are merely by how we perceive the problem. We have all met folks who can take an insignificant problem and make it appear as though the end of

WE CHOOSE TO MAKE THINGS MUCH WORSE THAN THEY REALLY ARE MERELY BY HOW WE PERCEIVE THE PROBLEM.

the world is very near. The frame is much larger than the picture requires. They present it in such a way that if there were an award for true-life drama performances, they would surely be nominated for best actor. When I meet those people, my first thought is that they lack resilience. They are easily knocked down by the slightest punch that life throws at them. I do not mean that in an unkind way or intend to be uncaring or uncompassionate. People are like they are for a reason. I must admit that those folks drain my energy. They constantly need support, and they rarely attempt to get better on their own. Much of their dilemmas lie in how they choose to view the problems they find so debilitating. When it comes down to it, they would rather talk about the frame than the picture, searching for sympathy instead of a solution.

Then there are those who allow the picture to diminish the room in which it hangs. The picture should take up only a small amount of space. It should not dominate the room or draw attention away from all the other great furnishings within it. Contentment in life is often based on how we choose to view it. If we allow the trial we face to distract us, we miss all the good things in our lives. Satan loves to give us tunnel vision in which we focus on one small aspect of life which has become challenging. We overlook the many blessings that are all around us. We face a financial challenge and forget that we are blessed with a job to help pay for it. We experience a bout of sickness or a scary diagnosis and lose sight of the time we have available right now to experience and express love to those around us. We struggle with an issue that seems out of our control but forget that we have a God who is able to do more than we could ever imagine (Ephesians 3:20).

Overcoming faith is all about having proper perspective. The portion of Scripture we have come to refer to as the "Faith Chapter" (Hebrews 11) begins like this:

OVERCOMING FAITH IS ALL ABOUT HAVING PROPER PERSPECTIVE.

Faith shows the reality of what we hope for;
it is the evidence of things we cannot see.
Through their faith, the people in
days of old earned a good reputation.
Hebrews 11:1-2 (NLT)

Faith is the evidence of what we *cannot* see. Much of what occurs in our lives is a result of what we cannot see with our natural eyesight. What we see is not all that is happening. In order to fully embrace our lives realistically, we must consider more than surface-level details. Otherwise, hope and faith are impossible. It sounds like a difficult task or even something that sensible people would not engage in. However, many of the world's greatest accomplishments came about as a result of having a perspective which goes beyond what is materially visible.

My wife and I took a trip to New Orleans a few years ago. During our time there we visited the National World War II Museum. It was an amazing experience. I highly recommend it to anyone who can visit. The display that had the greatest impact on me was one in which the armies of the conflict were illustrated by little toy soldiers in a glass case. Each figurine represented a certain number of soldiers. The contrast was stark. The odds of the allied forces winning the war against Germany and Japan were overwhelming. But the greatest weapon they had available was perspective. The future of a free world produced inner strength and determination to overcome. On the surface, the task seemed insurmountable. However, the thought of losing was unimaginable. Evil had to be overcome at all cost.

A trial is a conflict. It is usually an attempt by the enemy of our souls to entice us to lose hope and become discouraged. If we view it through the eyes of our natural limitations, the situation often seems hopeless. Satan wants us to focus on the few resources we have access to rather than the unlimited riches of Christ. Whenever we settle for flesh rather than faith, there is only one result — fear. That is Satan's ultimate goal. He wants to cast fear into our hearts. There is nothing much scarier than having to rely on ourselves as the only source of help in desperate circumstances. We know ourselves better than we know anything else.

Something happened to me one night during the trial we were going through. I was awakened by my wife going to the bathroom. Suddenly the Lord spoke to me very clearly. "The devil can't tell the future," He said to me.

I was startled. "What?" I asked.

"The devil can't tell the future," the Lord said again. "The only future he knows in what is written in the Bible," God said.

> "THE DEVIL CAN'T TELL THE FUTURE," THE LORD SAID AGAIN. "THE ONLY FUTURE HE KNOWS IN WHAT IS WRITTEN IN THE BIBLE," GOD SAID.

The next day I began to ponder on that message. I recalled the story of Job. The Bible declares that God began to inquire of Satan regarding his most recent activity. The devil proudly proclaimed that he had just been scouring the earth trying to find people to devour. Then the Lord said, "Have you considered my servant Job?" What followed was a tremendous trial for a guy who stood out as the picture of a solid man of God. Job soon lost his wealth, his children, and his health. He had done nothing wrong. He was the epitome of righteousness. Yet, there he was becoming the poster boy for suffering.

Job had no clue why any of this was happening. He struggled to understand why God had turned on him. His friends were convinced that he was being punished for secret sin that Job was unwilling to admit. His own wife encouraged Job to curse God and die (Job 2:9), but Job refused and hung in there. He struggled greatly as anyone would, but he maintained his character and faith. The funny thing was that God never told Job why the situation occurred. Job never knew that he was nothing more than an example of how faith can sustain a person through dire circumstances. The one thing that sustained Job more than all else was his perspective of God. He knew that God was good no matter what. Although Job never knew why it happened, in the end, God restored double what Job lost (Job 42:10).

I considered the story of Job in light of what the Lord told me that night. Satan did not have a clue how it was all going to end. In fact, he was certain that if he created enough havoc that Job would cave. The devil has a lot of tools, but he is at a disadvantage. He has no power over the outcome. God determines the end result and our perspective determines our outcome. If we look beyond the immediate and see things from heaven's perspective, we will always come out on top. God has never lost a battle. He is never taken by surprise or outwitted by Satan. Many people think that Satan and God are on the same level. Not true! God created Satan. Created beings are not on the same playing field as their Creator, even if they don't know it. No matter what havoc the devil wreaks, God has the uncanny ability to take anything bad and make something good out of it. It is like a chess game that always has one last move available. In the end, it's always God's turn to move the pieces. God is the King of Glory and Satan can never put Him in checkmate.

The message the Lord impressed upon me that night was a source of strength throughout the entire ordeal. Each time doubt tried to creep in, I was reminded that Satan only operates in the present and has no power over the future. He only controls what I allow him to have access to. If my mind is focused on the Word of God, he cannot rent any space in my head. I will not succumb to depression or fear if there is joy in my heart derived from knowing that I am a forgiven child of God. There will be no room for anxiety if I remind myself that God is in control. I kept telling myself that God has my back no matter what. My perspective was driven by the knowledge that God never fails and that He is always faithful.

SATAN ONLY OPERATES IN THE PRESENT AND HAS NO POWER OVER THE FUTURE.

What we believe about something determines how we respond to it. Faulty core beliefs cause us to buy into lies based on past experiences or messages that we have received from those we respect. If a man had three

WHAT WE BELIEVE ABOUT SOMETHING DETERMINES HOW WE RESPOND TO IT.

wives over time and each left him for another man, he might develop the faulty core belief that women can't be trusted. As a result, he may choose to deprive himself of the joy that comes from experiencing real love. If his "women can't be trusted" belief is never challenged, he will doom himself to a life of loneliness void of intimacy.

We make decisions daily based on previously acquired knowledge, beliefs, and experiences. We respond in ways that reflect what we believe about certain people, companies, or situations. Faulty core beliefs are associated with what we believe about ourselves. Perhaps we are hesitant to accept challenges because we recall times when we tried and failed. Lack of confidence stymies our potential. We may assume that things will always turn out the same. We employ irrational beliefs such as fortune telling. We predict the future even though it has not occurred yet. We sabotage ourselves before we even get started because we bought into lies.

> LACK OF CONFIDENCE STYMIES OUR POTENTIAL.

In 1991 my wife and I left Texas to come to Missouri so that I could attend Bible college. It was a step of faith. I had no job and didn't really know anyone in the area. The only work I could find was checking out groceries at a local supermarket for minimum wage. My wife stayed home to care for our one-year-old daughter. Times were hard, to say the least. I was trying to pay bills, tuition, and feed a family on a little over four dollars an hour.

Like most young couples, we had made some poor financial decisions early in our marriage. We tried every method possible to form a budget that would allow us to meet our obligations. It was impossible. I am no accountant, but I knew that at the very least I needed more income than outgo if we were going to stay afloat.

That luxury did not exist. Our bills clearly exceeded our income and my time was limited due to my schooling. I went to class in the morning, worked at the grocery store, and ran a rural newspaper route as well. Despite all my efforts, there was not enough steady income to give me confidence that we were going to make it.

My faith in those days wavered easily. I was still growing in the Lord and learning about God's faithfulness. My wife had been a believer since she was eight years old. Her faith was strong. I remember losing my composure once and telling her that it was impossible for us to succeed because the deficit was obvious. We could only do so much, and we had no support from those around us. I had a bill due that was $500 and no way to pay it. My wife said to trust God and that He would cause something to happen.

"How?" I asked. "No one even knows us!" I exclaimed.

"God knows us" was her calm response, "God knows everyone," she said.

I went to the mailbox to retrieve what I thought was typical junk mail. I threw it on the desk and went to a quiet corner to sulk. A few minutes later my wife sorted through it.

"What is this?" she asked. She had opened a letter from a newspaper company we had worked for in Waco, Texas before moving to Missouri. Apparently, they had been taking money out of my check each month as some sort of a surety bond and had sent us a refund. It was $500. That day I got a glimpse of God's economy and my perspective about faith changed. Over the next four years our budget never changed. Our income never exceeded our bills. It was an economic conundrum. However, we never once saw a bill go delinquent. We managed to graduate debt free. We even paid off the bills we had accumulated before coming to college!

A faith perspective is based on spiritual insight rather than physical eyesight. When we consider God's resources, strength, and power, our vision goes beyond our worldview. Although we cannot see the spiritual realm, it is just as real as the physical realm, and much more influential to the outcome. We cannot see air, but if it wasn't there or was toxic, we would perish. Operating in faith insulates us from toxic physical reality and gives us peace and confidence.

> A FAITH PERSPECTIVE IS BASED ON SPIRITUAL INSIGHT RATHER THAN PHYSICAL EYESIGHT.

In 2 Kings chapter six, there is a story about perspective. The king of Syria was attempting to overthrow Israel. Each time he planned an attack it was thwarted. The king had more firepower than the prophet Elisha, but Elisha had the upper hand. Why? Because God eliminated the element of surprise. God told Elisha what attack was coming, and Elisha warned the king of Israel.

Of course, the king of Syria was baffled as well as incensed. The king thought that he had a traitor in his camp. He soon learned that the person working against him was Elisha who had a hotline to heaven. He was determined to put an end to this leaker once and for all. He went to visit Elisha and brought a huge army with him.

The next morning Elisha's servant went outside to stretch his muscles in the morning light. He discovered that they were surrounded by thousands of enemy soldiers. I can picture the look that young man must have had when he saw the impending doom staring him in the face. He quickly rushed in the house and interrupted Elisha's first cup of coffee. His cry was exactly the same as ours far too often. "What shall we do?"

Elisha's response had more to do with perspective than it did with forming an action plan or deciding which direction to run. Elisha calmly looked at the servant and said "There are more with us than there are against us." Then Elisha prayed that God would open this young man's spiritual eyesight so that he could get the real perspective of the situation. God did just that. Suddenly, the servant was able to see things the way God saw them. Surrounding the enemy army was a multitude of heavenly warriors with horses and chariots of fire. God had their back.

Elisha asked God to smite the enemy with blindness. He was then able to lead them straight to the king of Israel to do with them as the king saw fit. As a result, the king of Syria decided that attacking Israel was not such a great idea and ceased his campaign. God expects us to see things His way. In fact, the only proper way to view our trials and problems is through God's eyes. Our first response in the face of a trial should be to seek a heavenly perspective on the matter.

GOD EXPECTS US TO SEE THINGS HIS WAY.

Every great man and woman of God had to adjust their perspective before they achieved victory. Jonathon looked at his armor bearer and suggested charging an army all by himself because it just might be that God would intervene on their behalf. David faced a giant because it was a battle that he suspected God would want to win. Esther risked her life interceding before her husband the king because she felt that possibly this was her destiny. The odds were not in their favor. The situations seemed ludicrous and ill-fated. Yet they all overcame and saw the trial end in a way that not only established God as God but also showed them the benefits of being servants of the Lord Most High.

So how do we gain a proper perspective while going through trials? It begins with reminding ourselves of who we are in Christ. If He died for us, then He will fight for us. God does not intend to allow anything to diminish the victory we have in Christ. In the end, we always win. We have been destined to always triumph over our struggles. That last chess move is invariably in God's hands, and it will always result in checkmate of the devil.

IF HE DIED FOR US, THEN HE WILL FIGHT FOR US.

Secondly, we must determine the environment in which we choose to reside. Is it a place of faith and encouragement or one of defeat? What we allow through our ear and eye gates will determine our state of mind. Much of what occurs around us daily is out of our control, but we can establish healthy, faith-encouraging habits that counteract much of the trash that is regularly deposited in life. Choose to start your day early with a time in prayer and devotion in the Word of God. Feed your spirit each day with faith-building messages spoken by men and women who believe that God is still a miracle worker. Make Christian music your favorite form of listening entertainment. It comes in all styles, so there's no excuse not to. Interact as much as possible with those who are not only encouraging but also wise. Wisdom comes from experience. Drawing strength from those who have already been through some struggles provides the perspective

YOU DON'T ALWAYS HAVE TO LEARN EVERYTHING THE HARD WAY. YOU CAN LEARN FROM OTHERS.

you have yet to gain. You don't always have to learn everything the hard way. You can learn from others.

Finally, encourage yourself! Become a person of faith. Pray about everything and then leave it alone. Take time to imagine what your testimony will sound like when the trial is over. Choose to purpose in your heart that you will come through this test with an A+. Remember that your experience may be the source of strength for someone close to you who is observing the process.

Trust the process. Something great is being accomplished anytime God is at work. It never feels good when the hammer and chisel are being applied to our lives, but the end result will be an intricate creation by the Master Craftsman.

CHAPTER 7

TRUST

*God expects us to know Him well
enough to rest in His arms.*

"Don't you care that we are going to drown?" That was how Jesus was awakened one night as he was catching up on some well-needed rest. He had spent a good part of the day by the seaside teaching the many people who were following him around from place to place. Some followed for the teaching, some for the miracles, and some just for a free meal. It had been a long day. He was obviously exhausted. His lack of physical strength is evidenced by the way he was able to sleep so soundly in the midst of a raging storm.

After teaching that day, Jesus told his disciples to get into a boat with him and make their way over to the other side of the Sea of Galilee. It was early evening just prior to sunset. The "sea" was actually a freshwater lake about seven miles wide. The fishing boat was a vessel about twenty-seven feet long. It was big enough for Christ to find himself a comfortable spot in the back of the boat and lie down. He fully intended to sleep through the trip. He would need all his strength. What waited on the other side of the lake was a demon-possessed man who was literally off the chain. Jesus undoubtedly knew the demoniac was there and the challenge that He would face. He also knew that they would get there safely because he had received His instructions from His Heavenly Father.

Somewhere in the middle of that journey, something unexpected happened. A storm rose up. Mark described it as a "great storm" (Luke 8:23). The Greek words used are **megas lailaps.** It doesn't take a Greek scholar to figure out the first word. It is the word we get the word *mega* from. So, Mark indicates the storm was not small in size or intensity. The second word is only used three times in the New Testament, and two of those occasions refer to this event. The word **lailaps** is defined in the Thayer's Dictionary as a violent attack of wind with furious gusts and floods of rain throwing everything topsy-turvy (Thayer and Smith, 1999). This would not be favorable circumstances for a pleasure cruise. In fact, the storm was so great that seasoned fisherman were, as we say in the South, scared spitless.

Several of the disciples had made their livings on that lake. It was not their first rodeo. Yet, we see these guys totally freaking out and convinced that they were going to sink. I have always found it interesting that their response to the trouble far too often looks a lot like our own when we face an unexpected trial. In Matthew, Mark, and Luke, each writer expressed impending doom with different words, but all are afraid. The first thing they did is what we usually do. They tried to fix the problem using their own intellect, resources, and ability. In this case, they likely tried adjusting their course and lowering their sail. When things got worse, they began bailing water out of the boat as best they could.

The water was obviously coming in faster than they could get it out. That is when fear set in. Isn't that how it normally works? We find ourselves in a situation, and we do all we can to fix the problem ourselves. Once we have exhausted all our efforts, we start to panic and let emotion take over. We also become convinced that things are not going to end well. We have a picture in our minds of what the future resembles and it doesn't look good — we think we are going down, our ship is going to sink, and there is little we can do to stop it.

It is hard to have faith when we are afraid. As a matter of fact, it is impossible. The Bible declares that fear comes from the devil. Faith comes from God. We can't draw from both sources at the same time. We can acknowledge our fear and then choose to exhibit faith, but we cannot express faith and fear

FEAR COMES FROM THE DEVIL. FAITH COMES FROM GOD.

simultaneously. All we can do in the moment of fear is cry out for help. Thankfully, God answers prayer when all the faith we express is in the belief that God exists and that we can depend on Him to come to the rescue. He often answers in that time of trouble and meets the need. But is that the way He expects us to respond? Is he pleased with us trusting in ourselves to the point we recognize that our efforts are futile and then as a last resort crying out to Him for help? The rest of the story answers that question.

As the disciples frantically tried to figure out what other means they might have available to save themselves, they remember one very important fact. Jesus is in the boat with them. They had gotten so involved in bailing water and turning rudders that they completely forgot that the Son of God was a few feet away. Somebody wakes Jesus up and cries for help. The result is that Christ stands up, lifts His hands, and says "Peace, be still" (Matthew 8:26, Mark 4:39, Luke 8:25). The wind ceased, the rain stopped, and the water became calm. The disciples marveled that even nature is subject the will of Christ. Lesson well learned, right? Wrong.

Jesus does not praise them for having the wherewithal to remember that their supernatural "spare tire" was in the trunk. He does not chide them for waiting so long to ask for help either. Instead, he asks them a couple of questions. This situation became *Discipleship 101* for his students and a perfect opportunity for a pop quiz. The first question seems a little out of line: "Why are you so fearful?"

Are you kidding me? The disciples are in a boat in the middle of a lake in the middle of the night and in the middle of a furious storm. Where does Jesus get off asking a question like that? Anyone in their right mind would have been concerned about his or her welfare and safety. Why would Jesus challenge their courage in such a way? Surely, he knew that at least a few of these men were not by any means timid. Peter, James, John, and probably Andrew were acquainted with the life of a fisherman. They spent their days repairing their nets and boats and their nights on the water. Peter was extremely impulsive, but he was not a coward.

The first question seemed to challenge their manhood. The second question challenged their spirituality. "How is it that you have no faith?"

No faith? None at all? Really? After all, these guys had all left their previous means of income and risked extreme ridicule as well as financial stress in order to join a profession for which none of them had any training. They appeared to be all in. They had some room for growth but to imply they had no faith at all seemed a bit harsh. Couldn't Jesus have been just a bit more sympathetic to their plight? They were in the very beginning of their journey with Christ. You might expect that Christ would grade their faith on a curve since the ministry was just getting launched. However, the words were clear, and the rebuke was strong. Jesus pointed out clearly that they had no reason to express fear and they showed no faith in their response to the trial.

God used this story during my recent time of testing to show me something I had never seen before. As I pondered the questions associated with his rebuke of the disciples, a couple of truths were revealed. The first is that our faith should not be based on what Jesus can do. Our faith should be based on who He is.

A leper came to Christ in the first chapter of Mark and said, "Lord, if thou wilt, thou canst make me clean" (Mark 1:40).

Jesus replied, "I will; be thou clean" (Mark 1:41).

This was a key lesson the disciples were privy to. The man knew that Jesus had the power to cleanse him from his incurable disease. That question was not on the table or up for discussion. The question was whether Jesus would have compassion enough to heal him. The answer was a resounding "Yes!"

The biggest mistake the disciples made in that boat was not mustering enough courage to ride out the storm. Their biggest mistake was questioning the love Christ had for them. They lost sight of God's nature. Their focus was on the intensity of the storm rather than the depth of His love. Trust is based on the character of the person you are placing faith in. Their ability can fall short, but their character will always ring true. The disciples needed only to remind themselves that they were in the care of the loving Son of God who would always have their best interests as His top priority.

I have learned that I cannot always predict what God will do. I would love to pray for a cancer patient and proclaim without a shadow of a doubt that cancer will flee and that they will recover. I cannot do that, and neither can anyone else. If they tell you they can, they are lying. I can pray with faith that they will be healed based on the knowledge that God is able to do what I ask. I can proclaim that I have no doubt that Christ is the Great Physician and that He can speak that disease into nonexistence if He so chooses. I cannot say without a doubt that it will occur. Only God knows that.

I may not be able to say I know what God will do, but I can say without one shred of doubt that I know who God is. He is a God of love. He is a God of wisdom. He is our Heavenly Father who views His children as an extension of His only son Jesus. He is a Master that takes good care of His servants. He is a Shepherd that never ceases to care for His sheep. He is perfect in every way, and His goodness never varies in any fashion. He is and always will be faithful. He never fails. He doesn't make mistakes. He is never caught off guard or surprised. He is more powerful than anything that has ever existed or ever will be devised by Satan or anyone else. He only does what will result in something that brings Him glory. That I can say without any doubt whatsoever. This is where the disciples failed.

We do not have to be Christians for a long period of time to know the character of Christ. We became fully acquainted with it the moment we experienced God's transforming love in our lives. It is as if a newborn child is laid at the breast of its mother for the very first time. The feeling is obvious. The devotion the mother has for that child is undeniable. Attempt to rip that baby from her arms, and you will witness the affection she has in the form of fierce opposition. Long before that baby was a fetus, it was first a dream that she had as a little girl. Later as the child was growing in her womb, she often thought of what it would be like to embrace her son or daughter for the first time. She knows that child is as much a part of her as the other members of her body. Nothing is going to separate her from the love she has for her offspring. She would willingly die to protect that child. God feels the same way about His children.

Jesus did not question the veracity of the storm or the seriousness of the situation. He was not upset because they interrupted His rest. He rebuked them because of their words. "Don't you care that we are going to drown?" Here is the basis for the indictment brought against the disciples. They were not questioning His ability. In fact, they woke Him up because they had some level of faith that He can rescue them. They were not questioning that He was the Son of God. They had already seen enough in their experiences with Him to convince them that Jesus was the Messiah. They doubted His character. "Don't you care Jesus?"

As a counselor, I have dealt with many couples who have experienced infidelity in their marriage. Occasionally I run across a marriage that is being deeply threatened by a failure that occurred years prior. The offended partner usually proclaims through teary eyes that in spite of the time that has elapsed, he or she just cannot trust the partner. They say that they have forgiven, but trust is destroyed, and they cannot get it back. The offender may have spent the previous ten years trying to recapture that trust but is now frustrated that, in spite of all the effort, success is no closer than at the beginning.

That is when I try to take time to explain how trust really comes about. The notion that someone can regain trust is a farce. Sure, the one who cheated must exhibit behavior that clearly indicates remorse and a change of heart. But ultimately trust cannot be earned. It must be given.

TRUST CANNOT BE EARNED. IT MUST BE GIVEN. It is based on what you believe about that person deep in your heart of hearts. It is as if your teenage daughter tells you she was spending the night with her friend Suzy, but you learn that she was really out with that boy you despise. She has broken your trust. How does she regain it? She may make a statement of recommitment. There may even be a time trial of sorts. Eventually, the trust will be restored because you believe in the character and nature of your daughter. You know that deep down she is a good person who deserves to be trusted.

If we can place that kind of trust in a fallible human being that we know has failed, we should have no trouble trusting Jesus. The disciples had spent enough time with Christ to know His character. They had felt His love in the way He accepted them in spite of their sins. They had seen the show of compassion He demonstrated in reaching out to the outcast leper and others. They had witnessed how He responded to the opposition of the religious leaders and even His own family members. They had plenty to go on. We do as well.

I watched my youngest daughter and her husband go through a trial recently. She came over one day to help me paint the inside of my house. My heart was burdened for what they were experiencing. I wanted so badly to tell her how things were going to turn out, but I could not. However, the Lord gave me a word for her that was much more encouraging than painting a picture of a rosy outcome. I looked at her with tears in my eyes and said, "I do not know what God will do, but I do know God." That is enough. That's all we need in the time of our deepest struggles. We only need to remind ourselves who God is, and that God's nature and character are forever constant. That is what the disciples needed to remember. The words they spoke to Jesus regarding His apparent lack of concern stung much more than the driving rain on His face. The unfounded accusation that Jesus might not care about the disciple's welfare prompted the rebuke.

Let's consider how the disciples should have responded. Had they given some consideration to a few facts, their reaction would have been different. They could have ended this story with commendation rather than rebuke. Here are a few things they knew:

1. First of all, they knew that they were squarely in the center of God's will for their lives. I heard John Maxwell say once during a leadership seminar that the will of God is not always the safest place to be, but it is the best place to be. He used Paul as an example. Paul was most definitely careful to be in the will of God. He was redirected on more than one occasion when he wanted to preach the Gospel in a certain area or province. We know from his writings that though he was careful to be led of the Spirit, he often found himself in peril. He was beaten, thrown in jail, shipwrecked and stoned. However, he never doubted that he was exactly where God

placed him and would not have considered residing anywhere else. Jesus told the disciples to get in the boat. There should be some level of trust that comes from knowing that we are where God wants us in spite of the storm that emerges.

2. Secondly, we see in this passage that Jesus did not stop with the command for them to get in the boat. He also declared His intention. "Let us pass over unto the other side" (Mark 4:35). He did not say there would be no opposition along the way. He did not say that they would not have to exert some faith and effort to accomplish the task. He did say, however, that He intended for them to reach the other side of that lake. Trust must be based on what we know God's intentions are for us. We must walk forward in the face of opposition. The uncertainty that accompanies the future will always be present because we do not have the ability to see or live in the future. God resides in the future just as He resided in the past. In His world, there is no future because His will is already accomplished, and He knows it. That is why He can declare it with such certainty.

> TRUST MUST BE BASED ON WHAT WE KNOW GOD'S INTENTIONS ARE FOR US.

I am a licensed professional counselor. I did not know that this would be my fate. God gave me a vision of hurting people being helped outside the walls of the church. Many people who need divine intervention are hesitant to walk into a church because of the fear of being judged or other reasons. One morning at 3:30 a.m., the Lord imparted to me a vision of a place in our community where people could come and get spiritual guidance outside of the church. He gave me a name: *Truth in Action*. That same day He led me to a three thousand square foot building on the Main Street of my town. Within three days, I was told that I could rent it for one hundred dollars per month for the first one year. Five years later, over fifty souls had come to the Lord. As a result, I was still paying one hundred dollars per month.

During the time I was volunteering in this fashion, God placed a desire in my heart to do more. A former student I had taught in Bible college stopped by one day. He became a teacher for a moment. He challenged me to further my education and pursue state licensure. I only had one problem — I was a convicted felon. In 1980, I had racked up eight felonies and numerous misdemeanors due to my drug addiction. Master's degrees do not come cheap. They require a lot of work and a good amount of cash. After all the schooling comes the state licensure test and finally the approval by the State Board of Professional Counselors.

I made a phone call to Jefferson City, Missouri to inquire about how my criminal record might affect my ability to be licensed. I was told that there was no way to know if I would be approved or not until I had achieved my degree, taken the national exam, and applied for a license. This could have produced some serious uncertainty except for one thing: I was positive that Jesus told me to get in the boat and go to the other side.

I was working full time, pastoring a church, and had two daughters and a wife. For over two years, I drove three or four times per week from Noel to Springfield (about two hours) to school and back. Every waking moment was penciled in on a calendar so that I could fulfill all my obligations and still have time to spend with my family. Finally, graduation day arrived. Yet I still had not reached the other side.

The National Counselor Examination for Licensure and Certification (NCE) administered by the National Board for Certified Counselors (NBCC) was not easy. I had taken many tests in my life but none quite like that one. You usually have a fairly good idea as to whether you passed a test after you mark the last question. I was clueless about this exam. I could do nothing but wait and hope that the many hours I had studied would pay off. They did. I was so happy to get the letter stating I had passed. I am sure that for most of my fellow test takers that letter was a release from all the anxiety and doubt they had been harboring for the nearly six weeks prior to it arriving. They knew the wait was over and it was now smooth sailing.

However, for me, the waters were still choppy. Yes, I had managed to get the degree and pass the exam, but would the board accept me and approve my license? All of the time, money, and effort would be wasted if they looked at my past and decided that I was too big a risk to gamble on. I reminded myself that it was God who placed me in this boat, and it was He who set my sail and course. In the natural, I had feelings of anxiety, but underlying those emotions was a certainty regarding the character of my Lord. He never fails, He is never wrong, and He is always faithful.

I was with my wife the day I received the letter from the State of Missouri containing my license. Words could not express the joy and gratitude we both felt. I wanted to call the board and personally thank them for making this decision. When I did, they told me something that would have possibly been helpful to know at the beginning. I was told that in cases such as mine, the board usually makes allowances if the conviction is over twenty-five years old. I graduated in May 2005. My conviction date was May 5, 1980! That information would have been valuable to me perhaps in one way, but in another, it would not have been. Since I did not know, my faith and trust grew more than it would have otherwise.

There was one other fact the disciples should have considered above possibly all others. Jesus was asleep in the boat. Regardless of the intensity of the storm, He was not affected. He was at peace. As the disciples were frantically trying to regain their bearings the Lord was sleeping like a child in its father's arms. As I began to ponder this scene, I got a really crazy thought. Could not the disciples have been doing the very same thing if they had just trusted the Lord wholeheartedly? Is it possible to rest in the midst of a storm? I believe it is. In fact, I am of the persuasion that Christ would have been pleased if they had. I can't imagine Jesus waking up only to find twelve guys asleep soundly at His feet and suddenly asking, "Why are ye so fearful?" or "How is it that you have no faith?"

> JESUS WAS ASLEEP IN THE BOAT. REGARDLESS OF THE INTENSITY OF THE STORM, HE WAS NOT AFFECTED. HE WAS AT PEACE.

What if John had suddenly stopped bailing water and pointed out how peaceful Jesus looked when He was asleep? How different this story would have ended if he had said, "Guys, all this effort is wearing me out! I believe I will take a little nap." What if John made his way to the back of the boat, fluffed a pillow, and lain down next to his Lord and Savior? Perhaps the other eleven would have taken the cue as well. Suddenly the boat that was tossed so violently would have become a big rocking cradle for a bunch of burly men. After all, why should they be worried if Jesus wasn't?

That scene may seem a little farfetched. It's not the usual way we tend to deal with life's problems. But maybe it should be. As I was muddling through my trial, the Holy Spirit kept reminding me that Jesus is not only in the boat with me, but He is resting peacefully. If He is not concerned, I shouldn't be either. All the anxiety and panic I could muster was not going to change the outcome. It was not going to nullify the fact that I am in the care of a loving Savior who is not about to allow my boat to go under because He is in it with me.

I went fishing once on Lake Livingston in South Texas when I was about eleven years old. A man that my dad knew invited me. We arrived at the lake, and to my surprise, there was a small rowboat for us to use. We were having a great time when seemingly out of nowhere dark clouds began to appear. Within moments they were upon us. The calm water had turned violently choppy. It was the first time I had ever been in a boat or in the middle of a lake in a storm.

Rowboats don't move that swiftly, especially when you're going against the current. The small boat we were in did not feel very safe. I felt fear start to creep up, and my heart started to beat rapidly. Then I noticed something. The man who was rowing the boat did not seem the least bit concerned. He rowed with the same pace he had employed earlier. His facial expression did not reflect fear. He looked composed and in control. Occasionally I could see a slight smile curl up one side of his mouth as we faced each other in the boat. It was pouring down rain, and the wind was blowing fiercely, but he did not seem frightened.

Later that afternoon, I heard him talking about the event to someone in another room. He described how surprised he was that the storm occurred given it was not in the forecast. He described his concern. Someone's child had been placed in his care, and he felt a great deal of responsibility. He talked about how he knew that it was essential that he remain calm and project peace and safety to me because he could see the fear in my face. He described how he had to control his emotions intentionally. I was shocked! I would have never known he was the least bit worried. I have to add as well, that his name was James. It probably wasn't his first rodeo either.

If a mortal human being can project peace to a frightened child, how much more can Christ calm our greatest fears? He is never caught unaware by a missed weather forecast. He is certain of the outcome. He is not caring for someone else's child. He is watching after His own. The peace He demonstrates is not a façade. It is genuine to the very core. The same peace He embodies is the peace we can experience if we choose to do so.

I genuinely believe that if all twelve of those men had determined that they needed sleep as badly as Jesus did, they could have all found a spot to lie down and rode the storm out. The result would have been the same, they would have arrived on the other side. Their efforts spurned by panic accomplished nothing. It was all a waste of time and energy. Their time would have been better spent regaining their strength via a good night's sleep. After all, Jesus was sleeping. That should have been their greatest source of faith. They needed only to trust the man they had left all to serve.

CHAPTER 8

COMMUNICATION

Faith must be fed daily through prayer and God's Word.

I sit with my laptop opened and my two "typing fingers" moving at the blazing speed of approximately twenty-five words per minute. My mind is hopefully moving a little faster than that. I have one goal in mind. That goal is communication. It is the only reason I am doing this. I desperately want to be able to convey to all who read this book what I believe God has placed in my heart. I do this because I believe it has value and that it could help someone at a time when he or she feels hopeless. I am convinced that what I share is inspired by the Holy Spirit.

I picture in my mind someone I love reading these pages and gaining insight and direction. Perhaps one day my grandson will find himself facing a dark trial, and his eyes will fall upon a dusty manuscript passed down to him by his Pa many years prior. As he reads the words, he feels that passion and senses that this was a labor of love written with a sense of urgency. He overlooks the unsophisticated writing style and sees the message. The words spring off the page as he desperately searches for some guidance amid his struggle. A phrase catches his eye. It finds its way to his heart. His spirit is lifted. The message counteracts his discouragement like some type of antivenom serum. Suddenly a fresh sense of hope begins to breakthrough like the sun out of the dark clouds of despair.

From that springs a passion for sharing my stories and the small amount of wisdom that I feel I have acquired throughout my life. All of us go through struggles and sometimes the most powerful thing we have available to us are words. Words can change our perception, thoughts, and emotions. They can cause us to reach down to the very bottom of our spirits and muster enough courage and determination to do what seemed impossible a few minutes earlier. Ask any mountain climber, marathon runner, or combat soldier, and they will tell you how powerful words can be.

When Nazi Germany was bombarding England in 1941, it appeared that the British Empire was sure to fall. A man many considered to be unsuited for the leadership position he had been given said these words,

*"Never give in! Never give in! Never, never, never – in nothing great or small, large or petty.
Never give in except to convictions
of honour and good sense."*
(October 29, 1941, speech given at Harrow School,
a boy's boarding school in Harrow, London, England).

Those were the words that inspired the people of England as well as the rest of the Allies to overcome what seemed like an insurmountable force and to defeat evil. It did not change the odds or the scope of the problem. It changed the level of determination that England exhibited to refuse to give in to the idea of surrender. The rest is literally history. That man was Winston Churchill.

Communication is a big thing with God. In fact, it is essential. It is the means by which an infinite, all-powerful, all-knowing supernatural being interacts with a frail, finite, mortal human being. There is little that takes place in the Bible that does not include communication between God and man. Much of that communication occurs at times when things are not going well.

> COMMUNICATION IS A BIG THING WITH GOD. IN FACT, IT IS ESSENTIAL. IT IS THE MEANS BY WHICH AN INFINITE, ALL-POWERFUL, ALL-KNOWING SUPERNATURAL BEING INTERACTS WITH A FRAIL, FINITE, MORTAL HUMAN BEING.

- God spoke to Noah when the world, in general, had already gone to pot, and we hadn't even made it out of the Antediluvian (pre-flood) stage yet.

- God spoke to Moses when an entire nation was enslaved in Egypt, and its future was in the hands of one wicked ruler who had little regard for their divine destiny.

- God spoke to Joshua when the nation He delivered faced their first big battle on the east side of the Jordan River and were ill-equipped, outnumbered, and inexperienced.

- God spoke to David when his entire city had been burned, all the goods stolen, the women and children kidnapped, and his own men wanted to kill him.

- God spoke to a little boy named Samuel because no other so-called prophet in the land of Israel was even listening.

The list goes on and on. God can speak to us at any moment. He often speaks when there is a problem.

Recently, Vice President Mike Pence was attacked by a liberal television personality because he indicated that God speaks to him (Joy Behar, *The View*, February 19, 2018). Those who do not have a relationship with the Lord have no understanding of how common this is for a believer. It would be impossible for Christians to be successful in understanding and fulfilling God's will for their lives without divine communication. It starts with an awareness of what God has spoken already in His written Word. It extends beyond that to the very personal and ongoing interaction Christians experience through the ministry of the Holy Spirit. Jesus declared to His disciples:

But the Comforter, which is the Holy Ghost,
whom the Father will send in my name,
he shall teach you all things, and bring all things to
your remembrance, whatsoever I have said unto you.
John 14:26 (KJV)

That would be an impossible task without communication.

On several occasions, I have posed a question to various audiences. I like to poll to see how many in the crowd feel that they have personally received a specific word or message from God in the last year, month, and week. It is amazing to me that in fairly large congregations, perhaps half indicated that they had heard from God in the last year. As the time frame narrowed, the numbers dropped drastically. This is concerning because our Christian experience is relationship-based. It is not dependent on ritualism or rule keeping. It wholly rests on our vibrant daily involvement with Christ.

Can you imagine a marriage in which there is no communication? Each day you just do what you assume is expected, but never take time to hear what your partner might be feeling or needing from you. You are never made aware of anything that displeases them. You are clueless about their hopes and dreams for the future. You are cut off from the intimacy that only occurs when one heart is shared with another. That marriage, if you could call it that, would consist of two very unhappy and disconnected people. A marriage like that wouldn't stand the test of time and would likely end in divorce. Yet, this is how many interact with Christ each day. They wonder why they are unhappy and unfulfilled. They feel Christianity is a letdown. They feel cheated because their lives never seem to get better, and they continue to fall into the same old traps. The problem occurs because they don't communicate with God.

If our interaction with God is essential to growing in Christ, how much more do we need to be plugged in with the Holy Spirit in the middle of a trial? If I am trying to navigate up the side of Mount Everest, I most definitely want to be within earshot of the guide that has already been where I am going. God knows the path we are trying to navigate through. He has the words of encouragement that will lift our spirits when we are about to throw in the towel. He is the teacher who is using the trial to school us.

We must be able to get the information He is conveying clearly and concisely if we are going to make the grade.

In 1996, I attended a series of open-air church services that we often refer to as Camp Meetings. I arrived on a Monday and several other pastors and I were having lunch that had been graciously provided by our hosts. We were engaging in usual preacher conversations about our ministries and congregations when the host pastor looked at me with a very serious look on his face and asked, "Why did you come here?"

That was sort of a weird question to ask. I looked at him with just as serious a demeanor and responded, "I came to hear from God."

"Then that is exactly what is going to occur," he replied.

He didn't know how desperate I was to hear God speak to me. For the previous three years, my wife and I had served as pastors at a church few would even consider. There was no money and lots of drama. Yet, we felt God had placed us there, so we stayed. It had been a tremendous struggle, and we had just gone through a very hard situation. Financially, we were broke. We knew that a change had to occur, but we were not sure when to leave or where to go. We had always been committed to the idea that unless we heard specifically from our Commander, we were to stay at our post. But winter was coming, and the provisions were slim. We would not make it unless something changed quickly.

I was planning on leaving the meeting Friday morning. By Thursday evening, I had received no more direction than when I arrived. The Thursday evening service began with Holy Ghost-anointed singing and worship. People slowly began moving towards the front of the open-air tabernacle and knelt to pray. It wasn't long before I found myself face down on a concrete floor crying out to God for help in our situation. I had taken four days off of work, and this was the last service of the week for me. The thought of returning home to my wife and two small children without a game plan to survive was sickening to me.

Suddenly I felt a hand in the center of my back, and it lingered there gently but firmly. I thought someone must have decided to pray for me, but no words were ever uttered. I began to break in my spirit. It was at that moment God initiated a very personal conversation with me — one like I had never experienced before and never again. I began to receive a very clear message in my mind giving very specific instructions. I was given the name of a man in Texas that attended the church my in-laws went to each week. I was told that I should move there and submit to his authority. He was in the process of renovating an old welding shop so that it could become a private Christian school. The Lord told me to go there and help him in any way I could. This was not something I had previously considered. In fact, I did not even know the man other than his name and face.

After receiving those instructions, I was given the opportunity to ask God questions that I wanted to be answered. I asked Him why He sent us to a church He knew would not grow. He told me that God places a high premium on faithfulness. He said He had tested me and found me faithful. I posed other questions as well, all of which He answered. Three times He told me to get up and dance for joy because He had given me the Word I had sought. Two of those times, I pleaded to just remain a while longer in His presence because it felt so good.

Finally, I did as He asked. I stood up and began to give God praise with all that was within me. As I was doing so, I heard another voice in my left ear. "That wasn't God," he said. "That was your imagination."

Just as quickly as I heard those words of doubt, the voice I had been conversing with previously spoke a Scripture reference in my right ear. It was a verse I was not familiar with. I won't explain further but let it suffice to say that I was hoping it was not some passage about how somebody begat somebody else! It wasn't. I saw a Bible sitting on a seat, and when I found the passage, it spoke directly to our situation. There was no doubt in my mind God had met with me.

Within two weeks we had rented a house over the telephone. We saw our new residence for the first time the moment our thirty-two-foot U-Haul rolled up in front of the house at about 11 p.m. My wife was not impressed. It needed a lot of work. Fortunately, that was one thing she had never been afraid of. I did exactly as I was told. The Lord blessed me with a good job, and within eight weeks, we owned that house lock stock and barrel. The school got built, and the Lord moved us on to our next place of ministry within six months. Everything He said came to pass.

There was one other thing God told me that night. He said He wants to meet with me like that every day. Are you kidding me? That was truly a once-in-a-lifetime experience. I have had God speak to me many times since but not in such a dramatic fashion. That is not the point. The point is that He *wants* to meet with me like that every day. What stands in the way of me taking advantage of that invitation is my willingness to set aside the time and make the effort to facilitate that meeting.

I learned that during times of trouble, God must have our attention. Often the trouble itself is a means God uses to command our attention. It is during times of struggle that we become super receptive to what the Lord might tell us through His word or the Sunday sermon that we only half listened to previously. I found myself searching for the mind of God as I navigated my way through my most recent trial. Prayer was not enough. I needed to hear the Lord speak to me. I needed that level of intimacy that only occurs when it is fueled by a deep-seated desire to connect on a deeper level. All my life I had heard the phrase "deep cries out to deep," but did not really understand its meaning until now. When we begin a journey to know God intensely, there is a gnawing hunger to be closer to Jesus that is never fully satisfied. Those events and activities that once seemed so important become nothing more than a necessary evil. I anticipated the next moment I would be able to spend alone with Christ.

At times, imagery can provide context in a way that words cannot. I read in the Bible where John laid his head on Jesus' breast at The Last Supper. John described himself as the disciple that Jesus loved. It wasn't that John was the Lord's favorite. God doesn't have any favorites. It was because John availed himself to drawing as close to Jesus as he possibly could whenever he saw the opportunity to do so. I can imagine John being the guy that walked beside the Lord whenever possible. If not able to be by His side, he was probably content to be one step behind. Whenever Jesus was thirsty or hungry, I could see John hurrying to the nearest well to fetch a drink or gladly offering his piece of bread because suddenly he wasn't hungry anymore. John had a heart for God.

A good shepherd loves every sheep in his flock. But the one that gets patted on the head or petted the most is the one that parks himself at the shepherd's side and constantly eases its head under his hand. That was John. I began to visualize myself lying on the chest of Jesus. I began to think about the benefits of doing so. I can hear His heartbeat. I can feel His breath on my neck. I can feel His touch. And most importantly, I can hear His whisper. That is where we should long to reside. The turmoil that rages outside can never match the inner peace that accompanies that level of closeness to Christ. It is sad that it takes turmoil to drive us to seek God's heart, but too often that is the case.

Famous British preacher John Bunyan was a Puritan man of God who lived in England in the 1600s. He is best known for his 1678 Christian allegory, *The Pilgrim's Progress*. It was published nearly 400 years ago and has never been out of print. Available in over 200 languages, *The Pilgrim's Progress* is thought to be the best religious literature to come out of England.

John Bunyan was placed in prison for over twelve years because he refused to stop preaching the Gospel. During that time his daughter died. His wife and family lived in poverty because he was not there to support them. Finally, he was released. Several years later, he returned to the Bedford jail where he had been incarcerated and made a strange request. He asked the head jailer to allow him to be placed back in the damp cell in which he had been confined. The jailer was obviously surprised and perplexed. He asked why he would ever want to visit that place again after all the hardship he endured there. "Because it was there that I felt closest to God," Bunyan replied.

How important is communication with God? It is essential. We only have three forces that influence us and our decisions. The first is Satan. While he is nothing more than a fallen angel and is not omnipresent, he certainly has an army of demons working overtime to place thoughts in our minds. These thoughts are designed to discourage and cast doubt on who God is and who God says we are. Those thoughts can be debilitating when we are facing uncertain outcomes. The devil only has a few weapons at his disposal. At the top of his list is negative influence. Satan is the father of all lies, and there is no truth in him (John 8:44). Everything he says is a distortion or the opposite of the truth.

The second force we encounter is our carnal nature or what we often refer to as our *flesh*. The Bible tells us that in the flesh dwells no good thing (Romans 7:18). It also states that when we are operating in the flesh, we cannot please God (Romans 8:8).

What does it mean to operate in the flesh? It means we trust in ourselves and our own insight and intellect rather than depend on the guidance that God offers us through the ministry of the Holy Spirit. That guidance cannot occur without communication. Prior to coming to Christ, we are ignorant of the help He offers. If we continue to lean on our own understanding after becoming spiritually aware, we move from ignorance to foolishness. We should know better.

The third force that can affect our actions and thoughts is God. He desires to lead us. He is our heavenly Father and has every intention of getting us through the trials of life as quickly as possible. As this book illustrates, the trial has a purpose. It is designed to help us to grow and gain wisdom. Like John Bunyan, it may be the tool that God uses to draw us closer to Him. It might be a means through which we discover just how unfathomable God's love and grace can be. The decision to either listen to the devil or trust in my own ability, or to allow God to take my hand

and lead me is a no brainer. The first (the devil) is a deceiver; the second (me) is incapable. However, God is capable, doesn't make mistakes, doesn't lie, and doesn't fail. Why would we choose anything but the help He offers?

As we begin to listen for the voice of the Holy Spirit in our hearts and minds, it becomes very familiar. God knows everything. He doesn't limit His knowledge to the spiritual arena. He knows it all. He knows if that used car you are test-driving is a lemon. He knows if that guy you are dating is a Boaz or a Bozo. He knows how much that job with the salary increase will actually cost you in the long run. He knows what is in your distant future and what is just around the corner, or in my wife's case on one occasion, what is just over the hill.

> GOD KNOWS EVERYTHING.

My wife and I would take turns delivering newspapers on an eighty-mile rural route each day. One of the highways we traveled was lined with rolling hills. One day as she was about to enter the highway from a patron's driveway, she heard that voice of the Holy Spirit she had become so acquainted with throughout the years. It was not audible but strong in her mind and spirit. "Wait," he said. She looked both directions again and saw nothing. She was about to proceed when she again felt the Lord was prompting her to stay put. It didn't make any sense, for a second. Then like out of nowhere, two cars streamed over the hill to her right obviously racing one another. Both lanes were full. Had she ignored the prompting of the Lord she would likely have been killed or seriously injured.

Just prior to leaving the church I spoke of earlier in this chapter, I conducted a month-long tent revival. I wanted to make sure that

I had done all I could to reach the lost. A fellow minister parked his RV in our yard, and we took turns preaching every other night. During the day we would also fast, pray, and go out into the town and pass out fliers and Gospel tracts.

One morning as I spent my usual time with the Lord, God showed me the face of a lady who resided in our little village. I did not know her personally but knew who she was. I was pretty sure she knew me as well. I knew her name and where she lived. The Holy Spirit gave me a specific command to go and visit her. I recognized the prompting and, in my prayer, assured the Lord that I would go there that day. I was thinking possibly later in the afternoon.

"No," the Lord said, "Go first thing."

My friend arrived to pick me up, and I had him drive to me her house. The look on her face when she opened the door was one of surprise, but her reaction was an even bigger shock. She grabbed me by my hand and literally pulled me into her house. As soon as the door shut, her head fell on my chest as she embraced me. She began to weep. I was not sure what was happening. I was a little nervous and confused. I asked her what was wrong.

I quickly learned that her husband had recently been killed. He was a known drug dealer and they had been ostracized by all her family as well as the rest of the community. The funeral had occurred a day or two before, and no one had attended. She told me that she was so depressed that she felt life was not worth living any longer. She decided to give God a chance. She told God that if He really existed and truly cared about her, direct someone to come and see her that morning. Low and behold, who should knock at her door but a pastor! That is how important communication with God is. It is sometimes a matter of life and death.

Communication is the means God uses to encourage someone else who may be experiencing a struggle. The words you are reading right now were all birthed out of my own trial. Your misery becomes your ministry. As you develop the relationship that includes ongoing communication with God, you become a resource God can use to aid others. When my daughter was facing an unexpected downturn in her place of employment, I was immediately burdened. I found myself in my yard sitting on a picnic table inquiring of God why this was happening. She loved her job and had received commendation. Without notice, it seemed that she would soon be unemployed.

> AS YOU DEVELOP THE RELATIONSHIP THAT INCLUDES ONGOING COMMUNICATION WITH GOD, YOU BECOME A RESOURCE GOD CAN USE TO AID OTHERS.

As I prayed, I sensed the Holy Spirit bringing the words of an old Andre Crouch song to my mind:

> *I thank Him for the storms He brought me through*
> *For if I'd never had a problem*
> *I wouldn't know God could solve them*
> *I'd never know what faith in God could do*
> (*Through It All*, 1971, Light Records)

I quickly made my way over to where I knew my son-in-law worked to give him what I hoped would be a word of encouragement.

Of course, God did just what He told me. In a few weeks, she was on a new job and went less than a week unemployed.

The Bible is God's first means of communication. It is God's love letter to us and life's instruction manual. Much of the information we are seeking in times of trouble is found between the covers of that book. We need only to take the time to seek it out. We do not need a supernatural revelation when He has already stated in black and white, and sometimes red, what God's perfect will is for us. The stories contained in the Old Testament remind us that while man is not perfect, he is most definitely loved. God has our backs. He can bring victory out of the most hopeless of situations. Supernatural intervention is commonplace in God's world. We should expect a miracle if that is what is needed to solve the problem.

> SUPERNATURAL INTERVENTION IS COMMONPLACE IN GOD'S WORLD. WE SHOULD EXPECT A MIRACLE IF THAT IS WHAT IS NEEDED TO SOLVE THE PROBLEM.

Within the pages of the New Testament lie the instructions we need to conduct ourselves in the manner that God expects. He has imparted to us the knowledge necessary for us to view ourselves as well as Christ in a proper light. In reading the Scriptures, we are reminded not to worry. We are told that trials are just a means God uses to make us more like Him. We are encouraged that in the end, we will always come out on top because that is how He has planned it. We are taught how to tap into the true source of strength that is always made available to us 24/7. God's hotline is always open.

The Word of God is truly a primary resource for strength and encouragement, but God does not stop there. The Holy Spirit is also God. He lives inside of every believer, and He can speak at will. I know that many people shy away from that type of thought because of the possibility of falling into fanatical error. I have had some bad meals in my lifetime, but I still go to restaurants. Many today cheat themselves out of one of the greatest blessings offered to the believer simply because of misconceptions. The book of Acts records numerous accounts of men and women being filled with the Holy Spirit and speaking in an unknown language. It is a real experience, and it is for every believer who has a desire to receive it. Once it occurs, the line of communication to God becomes much more obvious. It does not become more available because it is not a prerequisite to hear from the Lord. God spoke to a donkey on one occasion. He can speak to anyone he desires by whatever means He chooses. He is God.

Once I had received the baptism of the Holy Spirit, I began to experience a more intimate relationship with the Lord. I began to see things in the Scriptures that I would have previously skimmed past. I began to feel a deeper concern for the lost. I could sense the Lord giving me direction more often. I became much more familiar with the voice of God. I was not any more saved than before, but I was more aware of how saved I was.

WHEN YOU ASK THE LORD INTO YOUR HEART, HE BECOMES A RESIDENT, BUT WHEN YOU ARE BAPTIZED IN THE HOLY SPIRIT, HE BECOMES PRESIDENT.

When you ask the Lord into your heart, He becomes a resident, but when you are baptized in the Holy Spirit, He becomes President. I urge every believer to receive this free gift so that their communication with God will become more frequent and familiar.

CHAPTER 9

MEMORY

*Faith is enhanced by remembering the
many times God has proven Himself.*

Ihave a good memory. Well, actually I have a good long-term memory. I'm afraid that extensive marijuana use in the seventies and eighties likely took its toll on my short-term memory. That's why I usually put my deodorant on at least two times when I dress. I can't recall if I just did it or not. However, my long-term memory is quite amazing. I am sixty-one years old, and I can remember when I was two or three. I can't remember everything of course. I can remember certain people and events that made an impact on me. For example, I distinctly remember my very first friend. He was a little boy named Charlie. If I try really hard, I can get an image of his face.

One of my earliest memories came when I was still in diapers. I was looking under a lampshade that sat on an end table when I saw something shiny. It was gold and seemed to cry out to be touched. I remember reaching my small hand up under the shade and grasping for the object much like Gollum in *Lord of the Rings* trilogy *(Fellowship of the Ring,* New Line Cinema, 2001*).* I had to have the "precious." It seemed to have a hole in the top of it just big enough to place my tiny little fingers. It was at that moment that I became acquainted with electricity. I had inadvertently placed my fingers in the light socket. This is how I know I was so young. It was my diaper that cushioned the blow as I was knocked on my little toddler behind. A harrowing experience indeed but one I never forgot. It was also a lesson well learned. I do not recall ever doing that again.

Memory plays an important role in developing our faith. It can be the touchstone that we revisit time and again when we become discouraged or doubtful. The word *remember* is used 148 times in the King James Bible. All but twenty-seven of those occasions are in the Old Testament. This does not seem odd considering the relationship God had with Israel. If I didn't know better, I would tend to believe the Israelites must have grown up in the seventies as well. They were constantly forgetting what God had already accomplished and what He was capable of doing. They neglected to remember what they had been told or promised. They easily forgot that the consequences of their disobedience were devastating. Only a few days had passed since they had witnessed ten miraculous plagues in Egypt which allowed them their freedom before they began complaining. These people definitely had some short-term memory loss.

> MEMORY PLAYS AN IMPORTANT ROLE IN DEVELOPING OUR FAITH. IT CAN BE THE TOUCHSTONE THAT WE REVISIT TIME AND AGAIN WHEN WE BECOME DISCOURAGED OR DOUBTFUL.

Before we pass judgment on those folks, we should examine our own history. We live in a nation that God helped establish, maintain, and continues to bless. Yet, we see God being slowly pushed out of virtually every area of our lives. Christianity and godly morals are seen as the enemy of the masses and politically incorrect. God is seen as a myth that only weak-minded people embrace. As we watch immorality and violence escalate, we still refuse to acknowledge that we became a great nation because God was on our side, in our hearts, and protecting us. It was not our own doing. It was a result of God inspiring men of vision and courage to fight back against tyranny. It was God who enabled our forefathers to defeat England when the colonists were severely outnumbered and underequipped. We are truly one nation under God because His favor was upon us. For the most part, much of that has been forgotten. Memory loss can have devastating consequences. God expects us to remember.

Whenever there is a trial, we look to God to do something extraordinary. We often need a miracle. It would not be a trial if we expected things to work out on their own. We need the faith to believe that God is in control and that He will act on our behalf in the way He sees best. If I were to receive a diagnosis of terminal cancer, I would hope that amid the shock and awareness of the reality I faced, I would gravitate back to the benchmark of memories I had stored which reflect the power and goodness of God. He has already proven Himself faithful. He does not need to regain my trust or confidence in Him. It is not like we are starting fresh and I have nothing on which to base my faith. I just need to remember.

Begin at the beginning. If you are a Christian, you have already had at least one miracle occur in your life. He saved you. That was no easy task. First of all, Christ left heaven and took on the form of a human being and dwelled among us. He was born of a virgin. He lived a sinless life. He submitted to a horrible death on the cross in order to pay for our sins. He rose from the dead and ascended to the Father in heaven. He sent the Holy Spirit to draw you and me to the message of the Gospel. The Holy Spirit literally came into our lives when we asked God to forgive us. God Himself, in the form of the Holy Ghost, interacts with us on a personal level daily. That is a miracle like no other.

Perhaps like me, numerous other miracles were attached to that initial moment of conversion. I was a hopeless addict. I was bound by drugs, alcohol, and every other form of sinful pleasure you could imagine. Yet all that changed when Christ came into my life and God forgave me of my sins. If I had never seen another miracle or divine intervention occur in my life, I would still be convinced that God can do the impossible. What is your story? How did God orchestrate the events that brought you to the knowledge of Jesus? Who did God send into your life that He used to show forth His love or share the Good News of the Gospel with you? What occurred in your life to make you aware of the void in your heart that only Christ could fill? Nothing that occurred and no one that showed up in your life was a coincidence. They were sovereign acts of God and nothing short of the miraculous. Everything God does is supernatural. Do you remember?

If you have been living for Christ for a while, then you also have other stories to tell. One cannot walk with the Lord without seeing miracles. He purposefully leads us to the people and places where He is at work. It may have come in the

ONE CANNOT WALK WITH THE LORD WITHOUT SEEING MIRACLES.

form of answered prayer or the awareness that God strategically placed you in a specific place at a specific time. He does such things to build our faith. He wants us to understand that this journey we are on is Spirit-led.

I will never forget the first time I was used by the Lord. It occurred only a few weeks after I became a Christian. It was on a scorching hot July morning in Dallas, Texas. I was riding in the passenger seat of my dad's Buick Regal as we were on our way to church. We stopped at a red light, and a black man pulled up next to us in a sixty-something, beat up, pea green Impala. He motioned for me to roll my window down. I took notice that he was glistening with sweat. His hair was matted, and his eyes were red. His shirt was unbuttoned about halfway down his chest. I grew up in South Dallas and immediately I became suspicious of his motives. My street smarts told me to ignore him. But he persisted.

I pushed the button which allowed the window to come down and the nice cool air exited immediately. I almost sarcastically said, "Yeah, what do you want?"

"I saw your bumper sticker," he said. I had no clue what he was talking about. I had not paid attention to the back of the car that well.

"It says *Prayer Changes Things*," he said.

"So?" I asked expecting some negative slur about prayer or church to come next.

He then said "My name is Bill, I'm a heroin addict. I was wondering if you would pray for me."

I was wearing a new suit with a good haircut and enjoying cold air conditioning. I looked into Bill's desperate eyes and said, "I can do better than that, man. A month ago I was exactly where you are now, and God saved me."

"You?" he asked with shock.

"Yes, I was a heroin addict, and God saved me. He can do the same for you," I said.

Hope came into those empty eyes, and a smile came across his face. Suddenly the light changed, and we drove off. I wept for the next sixty miles because I knew that God could have sent Bill to most any red light on a Sunday morning in Dallas, Texas and he possibly would have pulled up next to a Christian on the way to worship. He sent Bill to me. He knew that Bill needed more than prayer. Bill needed a personal witness of God's delivering power. Bill needed something to remember, and so did I.

Most any trial I encounter these days is accompanied by a memory to build and maintain my faith. I sit here with many of those events flooding through my mind. Often financial trials strain our faith. I need only to look back over the many times He has provided in ways that were beyond my comprehension. I recall a time when I was in between semesters while attending Bible college. My wife was pregnant with our second child. We were the epitome of struggling college students. We had returned to Texas for the summer, and I had taken a job about sixty miles from where my wife was staying with her parents. I stayed at a pastor's house during the week and came home on the weekends. I was working as a laborer on a framing crew. I got up at 4 a.m. and traveled with the crew to Austin from Waco and returned late in the evening tired and discouraged. It seemed that no matter how hard I tried to save the five hundred dollars for the down payment on the next year's tuition, something stood in my way. By the end of the summer, it appeared that I had reached a place of defeat.

Every day at lunchtime I would make my way into a small patch of woods behind the house we were building. I would pray and read a small New Testament I carried with me. One of my co-workers was a youth pastor at a local church but for some reason took it upon himself to challenge my strong convictions and beliefs almost daily. Often, I would ride with him in the mornings to meet up with the crew. Those rides were sometimes filled with tension even though we were both believers.

Finally, my last day on the job arrived. I was no more prepared to pay my tuition than the day I started. A couple of weeks prior to that day, I had felt the Lord speaking to my heart from 1 Corinthians 15:58 that my labor was not in vain. I had also attended a church service one night, and the minister stirred my heart with a message of encouragement and faith and told me that I should not let go of my miracle. He had placed a small piece of cloth in my hand as a visible representation of the divine miracle I needed to occur. I kept it by on my nightstand at the pastor's house.

That last morning, I loaded my belongings up and made one more trip inside the house to make sure I had not forgotten anything. Nope, everything was in the car. My eyes fell on that piece of cloth on the nightstand. I made no effort to retrieve it. I walked out of the door in defeat telling myself, "So much for that miracle."

I met my obnoxious coworker thinking that at very least I would be rid of him and his ridicule. There was a silver lining after all. As we were riding along, he told me that he and his wife wanted to give me a little something to aid me in my endeavor. He handed me an envelope. I stuck it over the visor hoping it contained enough gas money to get my beat-up Chevy Chevette back to Missouri. I figured he must have felt bad about the way he treated me. Twenty or thirty bucks would take care of that guilt easy enough.

I got into my car after a long day of work and made my way to my in-law's house. I dreaded telling my wife what a failure I was. I contemplated how we were going to survive the next couple of months with one child already and another baby due in a few weeks. I lowered the sun visor, and the envelope fell in my lap. Curious, I pulled the car over to see what it contained. I tore open the envelope and took out the contents. I started counting: one, two, three, four, and five…FIVE one-hundred-dollar bills! No one on the crew knew how much money I needed. They were only aware that I was preparing to return to college. That miracle occurred twenty-six years ago. I will never forget it. Memories are important.

Perhaps the trial may involve physical sickness. I have no doubt that God heals the sick. My dad suffered for years from Meniere's disease. It is a disorder of the inner ear that causes violent fits of nausea at any given moment. I have witnessed him sitting quietly one moment, and then be suddenly lying on his back with the room spinning like he had just gotten on the Tilt-A-Whirl at a carnival. He would begin to vomit uncontrollably. If he was not rushed to the hospital, he would begin to dehydrate. They gave him medicine, but it didn't help much.

One day he was sitting in his small apartment and began to worship the Lord. There was no music and no preacher. There was only Dad and the Great Physician. He would tell us later that he began to feel something like warm oil flowing from his head over his body. He was surprised and verbally asked the Lord what was happening to him. He said the Holy Spirit spoke to him and told him not to be afraid. God was healing his body. My dad never took another pill, and he never experienced another symptom.

I recall a particularly difficult night when my youngest daughter as a baby wouldn't be comforted and cried incessantly. My wife stayed up with her and I went to sleep. Hours later, I woke up and heard the baby still crying as intensely as she had earlier. I didn't need a word from God to know that my wife was on her last nerve and needed me to relieve her. I took my child in my arms and urged my wife to go to bed. My little girl felt hot with fever. She was obviously in a lot of pain as well. There is likely no feeling quite as helpless as when your child is hurting, and you can't do anything to alleviate the pain. I began to pray and ask God what was wrong with my baby. I saw her began rubbing her ear against my chest. I carried her into the bedroom and told my wife what was ailing her. We both laid our hands on her and prayed that God would heal her. She immediately stopped crying and fell fast asleep. Despite what I had just seen, my faith was still lacking. I told my wife we would probably need to take her the doctor the next day. That trip was not needed. She woke up healthy and happy as if nothing had occurred. I will never forget it. Memories sustain us.

Sometimes the greatest memory we can lean on is a word the Lord has placed in our hearts. There are folks who believe that God does not personally speak to people anymore. Are you kidding me? I seriously doubt that God is going to allow Satan to do something that God Himself can't do. One of the devil's main goals is to tell us things that are untrue and contrary to God's will. Most of those well-meaning Christians that claim God has somehow developed spiritual laryngitis are often quick to disclose how much time and effort Satan has spent trying to discourage them through negative thoughts. Francis A. Schaeffer wrote a series of studies entitled *He Is There and He Is Not Silent* (Tyndale House, 1972). Dr. Schaeffer addressed philosophical questions and showed how through various periods of man's history, God has consistently made Himself known. He will continue to do just that.

Not all personal revelations are from God. Some people misuse "revelations" for their own benefit, and some of the supposed revelations might as well come off the back of a cereal box because they do not line up with God's Word, so they cannot be from Him. Just because there are those who abuse the concept of God speaking to man doesn't mean that God doesn't. He does and He will speak to you if you pursue a relationship with Him.

It is interesting that if I relay to you something the Lord has spoken to me, it does not sound all that earth-shattering. However, when the Lord speaks those words to you personally, the weightiness of the message is much more obvious. Sometimes it is just a phrase. Other times it is a specific command or even a rebuke if needed. The point is that when you know in your heart that it was the Lord who spoke to you, it is not easily forgotten. It may be a source of strength or encouragement that carries you through a long period of trouble. It may be a form of symbolism that reemerges in your mind from time to time when you become discouraged or doubtful about your calling. When God blesses us with a specific word, it is for a specific purpose.

Not long after I began preaching, I found myself discouraged. I had lost my job, and my wife was working at a furniture factory.

Few things are more disheartening than for a husband to be unemployed and his wife leaving for her job in the morning. I was also at the very beginning of my ministry and was having a hard time understanding how God was going to take me to a new level.

I was at home, so I decided that I should try to get as much housework done as possible while my wife was on her job. I was standing in front of the kitchen sink washing dishes when Satan decided to launch an attack. The words I heard in my head were not good: "You are an ex-con and ex-drug addict. You're nobody. You don't deserve to be a preacher. Look at all you have done in your past — you are nothing."

With each attack, my heart sank deeper into despair and shame. I literally began to agree with the enemy. "Yeah, you are right," I thought, "I am nothing."

Then the Lord spoke into my heart a few words that contradicted that entire onslaught, "Elisha was just a farm boy."

Now that may not sound very prolific. It misses the mark when it comes to earth-shattering news. I doubt it will ever make a cover story in *Charisma* magazine. But to me, it was a message that caused the sun to burst through the clouds of despair in a way that I cannot describe. The water level in the sink grew a bit from the tears that flowed as I stood there coming to grips with the fact that God can use anyone He chooses regardless of their past or their qualifications. That message has been a reminder to me numerous times over the last thirty-two years when I have been faced with uncertainty regarding God's call on my life or my ability to fulfill it. He only spoke it once, but I have never forgotten it. Memories are perpetual. It is just as fresh today as the day I experienced it.

The written Word of God is the greatest source of strength, guidance, and power that exists. It has survived thousands of years and has never been proven wrong. It is the ultimate basis for our faith for it declares that, "Faith comes by hearing, and hearing by the word of God." (Romans 10:17). God speaks through His Word. We should commit the Scripture to memory. Christ turned to the Word when tempted by the devil in the wilderness. If Jesus demonstrated to us that the Word was all we need to defeat the enemy of our souls, should we not emulate His example? The Bible declares that the Word of God shall not pass away (Matthew 24:35). It is eternal and will forever stand. It is essential that we have it committed to memory.

> THE WRITTEN WORD OF GOD IS THE GREATEST SOURCE OF STRENGTH, GUIDANCE, AND POWER THAT EXISTS. IT HAS SURVIVED THOUSANDS OF YEARS AND HAS NEVER BEEN PROVEN WRONG.

I read in Deuteronomy chapter six that the ancient Saints were told to keep the Scriptures before them at all times. They literally wore pieces of Scripture on their bodies. They wrote commandments on the doorposts of their homes so that they were visible when they came and went. They recited the law constantly. They personally taught the Scriptures to their children and spoke of them daily. It was as much a part of their daily life as eating a meal or drinking a cup of water.

Later Jesus taught that we should seek God daily for our daily bread (Matthew 6:11). Was He referring merely to our physical food? I don't believe so. He was endeavoring to impress upon us that we are helpless and weak without a steady diet of the life-giving Word of God. When we commit Scripture to memory, we have the most powerful concealed weapon that exists. At any given moment we can be attacked. However, Jesus told His disciples that when the time of testing and trial came, not to worry about what they would say. He told them that the Holy Spirit would bring to their remembrance what they should say and aid them in their response (Matthew 10:19-20).

I had a friend in Bible college named Robert. I have never met anyone who had a greater passion for personal evangelism. He would order Gospel tracts by the case. I would not be surprised to learn that during the four years we attended college there was not one person in our community who did not receive at least one Gospel tract from Robert. He loved to tell people about Jesus. If he saw a person walking down the street, he would turn his vehicle around and spend as much time as that unsuspecting sinner would allow sharing the Good News.

Robert had been a drug addict and an alcoholic. His mother was an alcoholic while she was pregnant with him, and his brain did not function normally. As we went through our classes together, I remember him receiving a B on a test we had taken. You would have thought he just won the lottery. It was the only grade I am aware of that he earned higher than a C. For Robert, a D was the new B. He had no memory recall. We often studied together. I would ask him the same question over and over and tell him the answer afterward. Less than a minute would pass, and he had already forgotten the answer. It was very sad to watch him struggle with his disability.

However, Robert committed himself to memorize Bible verses. He wrote each verse on a 3x5 index card and secured them all together on a large metal ring. They went everywhere Robert went. When he was in his truck, they hung from his rearview mirror. If you asked him to recite one of the verses, he would be very hard pressed to do so. However, I have personally watched Robert recite verse after verse, word for word when speaking to someone about their need to come to Christ. They were always in his heart. They were in his mind only when he needed them to be. God will enable us to commit His Word to memory if we put forth the effort.

Memory is a choice. We choose what we remember. As a counselor, I have encouraged many people to practice selective memory in a positive manner. I see no value in recalling the bad things I have done which only produce guilt and shame. I know that doing

MEMORY IS A CHOICE. WE CHOOSE WHAT WE REMEMBER.

so creates feelings of low self-worth and depression. The past is full of memories. Our mind is similar to a computer hard drive. We store the good along with the bad. We are the keypunchers. We have the power to bring to the forefront of our minds what we choose to recall. This can be a blessing or a curse. God wants us to use what we have at our disposal wisely.

Memory played an important role during my most recent trial. I often recalled how my business came into existence. It was not through my own doing. It was something God initiated. I reminded myself how I came to possess all that I own. It was all blessings from God. He is my source. I remembered the many times I had struggled in the past and how God always proved He was faithful. I remembered that there had not been one occasion in my Christian experience when our bills went delinquent and our stuff was repossessed. I reminded myself that this was not a trial I created because of sin on my behalf. It was not a consequence of my poor choices or bad behavior. Memories are powerful.

Perhaps as you read this book, you are facing a tremendous trial. I encourage you to utilize the weapon of memory. Take some time to recall all the Lord has done for you thus far in your life. Remember that we were never promised that we would not have to endure hardship. In fact, it is just the opposite. Jesus told His followers that they would most definitely face trials and trouble (1 Peter 4:12). But also remember that Jesus said to be of good cheer because He has already defeated the world and the devil (John 16:33). Try to remind yourself that every struggle has a purpose. Our goal is to come through it stronger and more like Christ. Remember that nothing takes God by surprise. Remind yourself that His love is forever constant.

There is no end to the truths that God wants us to remember.

*In the same manner also He took the
cup when He had supped, saying,
"This cup is the new testament in My blood:
this do ye, as oft as ye drink it, in remembrance of Me."*
1 Corinthians 11:25 (KJV)

Jesus knew that even though the disciples had seen and experienced much, they would have a tendency to forget. All else pales in comparison when we choose to remember Him. Memories are important.

CHAPTER 10

JOY

"Faith is fueled by the inner joy that comes from an intimate relationship with God."

The preacher slowly emerged from the comatose state he had been in for the past several hours. It was pitch dark. The smell of human feces and urine mixed with musty mold was undeniable. It was enough to make him wish he hadn't waked up at all. Yet it was all too familiar. He could hear water slowly dripping somewhere nearby. Someone was snoring. Someone else was groaning in pain. Still, another was cursing the day he was born. The cold, wet stone against his body told him he was partially naked. No wonder he was shivering. He tried to move. Intense pain shot through his body like a bolt of lightning. The pain was all too familiar. He had almost become accustomed to it.

Was this the fourth or the fifth time he had endured the dreaded 39 stripes save one? It really didn't matter. Each flogging came with its own unforgettable form of terror. He tried to remember how long he lasted before passing out from the torturous punishment. It was somewhere during the final two-thirds of the beating because he was receiving the lashes on his back. The first thirteen stripes are always administered on the chest. Those hurt the worse. By the time his back was being torn open like shredded paper, he was usually dissociated from his body. He would think about the possibility of this being the moment he gets to once again visit that heavenly realm he had been shown once before after a stoning left him dead for a bit.

He remembers his friend. He reaches out in the darkness and feels someone close to him. The body begins to stir. "Silas, is that you my brother? Are you still with me?" he asks.

There was a pause of silence, then the sound of a deep breath being taken, and finally a weak response. "Yes, Brother Paul, I'm still here."

"Praise God, Silas," the preacher responds.

"Our task has not yet been completed else we would be with our Lord right now."

"Would God that it was complete." Silas says weakly, "I don't know if I can endure such trouble much longer."

"Then there is but one thing that we should do, Silas," Paul says.

Another deep sigh could be heard coming from his comrade. "And peradventure, what might that be?" Silas asked knowing the answer already before he even spoke.

"We must give God praise! We must sing a hymn in honor of our heavenly Father who has chosen us to suffer for the name of His Son Jesus," Paul responded.

Silas was not surprised. It seemed that Paul did most of the preaching and Silas did most of the singing. Silas often wondered if that was the only reason that Paul brought him along. But sing they did, and as they sang, two things occurred. They felt the strength that accompanied the joy of the Lord, and God shook an ancient jailhouse to its very core.

There is a difference between joy and happiness. Happiness is a variation of the word *happening.* One is usually happy when something is happening. Once the happening is over, the feeling of happiness soon fades. Joy, however, is not dependent upon outward circumstances. Joy is a state of the heart that can be sustained in the darkest of times. It is not affected by the ups and downs of life. That is not where it comes from. Joy emerges from something otherworldly. Therefore, the world and all its tribulation cannot taint joy unless we allow it. Joy is like a fortress that is surrounded by walls of steel. It was designed to be that way because our greatest source of strength lies within those walls.

> JOY IS LIKE A FORTRESS THAT IS SURROUNDED BY WALLS OF STEEL. IT WAS DESIGNED TO BE THAT WAY BECAUSE OUR GREATEST SOURCE OF STRENGTH LIES WITHIN THOSE WALLS.

The Bible declares that the joy of the Lord is our strength (Nehemiah 8:10). If we seek faith to endure trials, then we surely need strength. If we need to be strong, then apparently joy is necessary. Where does joy come from and how do we obtain it? Is it always present in the life of the believer or is it one of those traits we must develop as we go along? The Bible declares in Galatians 5:22 that joy is a fruit of the Spirit. One thing we know about fruit is that it is a product of growth. However, in the case of joy, there is no waiting period required to feel its presence. There is only one prerequisite for it to emerge in our lives. That mandatory requirement is forgiveness. One cannot experience joy without forgiveness. Forgiveness is the womb from which joy is birthed into existence.

> **FORGIVENESS IS THE WOMB FROM WHICH JOY IS BIRTHED INTO EXISTENCE.**

I have had the privilege of leading a number of people to the Lord. There is no feeling that matches the joy I feel when a person bound by sin and discouragement asks God for forgiveness and accepts Christ into his or her heart. I have seen people from all backgrounds make that decision. Regardless of their past or present circumstances, financial state, race, or gender, one thing is common. Once the final *Amen* is uttered, a smile as big as Texas floods across their face. They do not have to be told to smile. They don't need to wait until they grow more in the Lord or attend a series of discipleship classes. It is a byproduct of the knowledge that they have been forgiven. Joy springs forth from forgiveness. I can also tell you from experience that when believers lose their joy, it is because of a lack of forgiveness.

I recall a lady who attended a church where I served as pastor. She professed to be a Christian and had a very sweet attitude toward others. She was always eager to serve in whatever way she felt able to do so. She was never rude or mean. She had just one problem. She had no joy. Everyone around her could be bursting with praise and worship, and Lisa would stand rigid as a board with as flat an affect as one could imagine. I knew that there was a problem that was unresolved in her life and I was determined to find out what it was.

I paid her and her husband a visit one evening and managed to engage her in some very serious conversation. I told her that I had been observing her for a while and that I felt that there must be some area of unforgiveness she was holding onto. She denied that there was, but then her husband spoke up instead. He urged her to share her story of past sexual abuse. She began to tell me how she and her sisters had been sexually molested by her father when they were children. Tears began to form in her eyes. "I have said for years that I forgave him," she said. "I guess saying those words only pushed the hurt and bitterness further into the recesses of my heart and mind." We prayed together and later I could see a noticeable change as she made the slow journey towards true forgiveness and the joy that accompanies it.

There is a feeling of joy that comes from knowing that everything between us and God is taken care of. Think back to the moment when you accepted Christ in your heart. Remember the sense of peace and comfort that seemed to envelop you once you realized your many sins were forgiven? Perhaps later in your Christian experience, you had someone hurt you or betray you. Maybe you, like me, had gone through a time when the sting of that wound lingered far longer than necessary. Slowly you made your way back to the cross where you placed the offense at the foot of the Savior who paid for every sin and purchased our peace. Then it happened. Joy once again began to emerge in your life.

Joy is like a mail carrier that brings with it a host of packages containing essential elements to victorious faith. It is impossible to experience overcoming faith without joy. Enduring faith is driven by our thoughts. Thoughts are a product of emotion. If our

> JOY IS LIKE A MAIL CARRIER THAT BRINGS WITH IT A HOST OF PACKAGES CONTAINING ESSENTIAL ELEMENTS TO VICTORIOUS FAITH.

emotions are not Spirit-controlled, our thoughts are going to reflect it. Let me give you an example of how that works.

I have a little catch phrase I use quite often. It's called *Happy, Helpful, Hopeful.* I am not sure how I came to the knowledge of this little tool, but I am certain it was inspired by the Holy Spirit. I use it whenever my thoughts begin to gravitate in a direction that is contrary to a healthy mindset. As a former drug addict and alcoholic, I am acutely aware of the negative impact that "stinking thinking" can have on me mentally, emotionally and spiritually.

For example, consider what occurs when a negative memory from your past invades your thoughts. Usually it involves something that is associated with guilt or disappointment. Immediately, feelings of regret, anger, or shame produce what can only be described as depression. Suddenly your mindset and outlook are determined by the rogue thoughts that have commanded your attention. However, consider for a moment what these thoughts really are. They are nothing more than memories. Memories are wisps of the past that can never be changed or altered. What's more, they are products of our own choice.

While I may not have initiated the bad memory, I certainly have the power to choose whether to continue to entertain it.

That is when I tell myself "Happy, Helpful, Hopeful." If I am going to concern myself with thoughts of the past, I should determine what those thoughts are. After all, they are merely memories. Why would I choose to dwell on a bad memory when there are so many great ones to choose from? I know depression accompanies the choice to recall my past failures or the wounds I have received from others. If I am willing to dedicate time to reminiscing about previous life events, then I choose to only entertain happy thoughts that contribute to the essential joy that brings me strength.

Negative thoughts about the future are usually associated with worry and doubt. If I consider the uncertainties of life, extreme anxiety is not far behind. People who struggle with panic attacks will be the first to tell you how quickly negative thinking can trigger the physical reaction of a pounding heartbeat and uncontrollable breathing. The funny thing is that none of it has happened yet and may never occur. It is a conjecture in our minds regarding a space of time that has not yet arrived. Most of the things we worry about never happen anyway.

Whenever I realize that my focus has gravitated toward anxiety-producing thoughts, I tell myself "Happy, Helpful, Hopeful." If I am willing to devote precious time considering the future, I prefer to dwell on something hopeful. After all, I have the power to choose what the future looks like inside my head. I like to imagine the pleasure I will gain from teaching my grandsons how to hit a golf shot or watch them drop their first deer. I love thinking about taking my wife somewhere we have never been. I smile when I think about holding the granddaughter I don't have yet. *The future is as bright as I choose to imagine it can be.*

Finally, there is always the present to consider. There are many forces that fight for our attention on any given day. There is no shortage of people who seem to make it their life's goal to mistreat you or drag you down. The news of the day is constantly filled with plenty of fuel for negative thinking. It is not difficult to develop an attitude that is cynical, sarcastic, or judgmental. It is during these moments I remind myself about "Happy, Helpful, Hopeful." Are my thoughts in the present helpful? Are they helpful to me as well as to others? Do they promote the plan and purpose of Christ or are they self- seeking? The thoughts I entertain at any given moment either contribute to my sense of joy or draw my attention away from it.

This is not some sort of pop psychology. The Bible declares what we should think about. Paul wrote a short letter focused mostly about joy to some folks in Philippi. He emphasized the need to align our thinking with the joy we possess. He suggested strong boundaries in our thought lives. Consider these verses:

Always be full of joy in the Lord.
I say it again—rejoice!
Don't worry about anything; instead,
pray about everything.
Tell God what you need,
and thank him for all he has done.
Then you will experience God's peace,
which exceeds anything we can understand.
His peace will guard your hearts a
nd minds as you live in Christ Jesus.
And now, dear brothers and sisters, one final thing.
Fix your thoughts on what is true,
and honorable, and right,

and pure, and lovely, and admirable.
Think about things that are excellent
and worthy of praise.
Philippians 4:4; 6-8 (NLT)

Joy is not only affected by our thoughts. It also drives our thoughts. Thoughts produce behavior. People who operate within the realm of joy are easy to spot. Their actions give them away. Joy often causes the unbelieving spectator to wonder in amazement at the response of joy-filled believers who are suffering through trials.

> JOY IS WITHIN ITSELF A SUPERNATURAL FORCE FIELD THAT SHIELDS THE BELIEVER FROM THE TYPICAL IMPACT OF TROUBLE.

They are hard-pressed to find them complaining. They seldom see negativity flowing from the life of the joyous Christian. At times it seems that joy is within itself a supernatural force field that shields the believer from the typical impact of trouble.

Those drawing their strength from joy often give God praise in the middle of the trial. Every trial makes them stronger. They are keen to the truth that in the end, all things will work out for their good despite the hardship they are enduring. They rejoice that as children of the King, they will always triumph no matter what is hurled at them. Joy is like the force that drives the jet above the storm clouds where the sun is always shining. It doesn't cause the storm to go away, but it does enable you to rise above it.

Joy produces a sense of gratitude. There is never a moment when we do not have something to give thanks for. We are blessed regardless of the trial we face. Consider the story of Corrie ten Boom in her autobiography, *The Hiding Place* (Haarlem, 1940).

After hiding Jews during World War II, Corrie and her sister Betsy were placed in a Nazi prison camp. The guards often sexually abused the women in the camp. However, the barracks that she and her sister were placed was infested with fleas. As a result, their captors refused to go inside. Corrie would pray and give thanks each day for the fleas which were a constant source of irritation, but definitely the lesser of two evils.

When struggling through trials, it is easy to focus on the problem rather than on all the good that is around us. Joy gushes forth when we see what the Father has already provided. We gain new energy when we recognize that the same God who has provided all the blessings that we currently enjoy is our one and only true source of help. He is not short on anything. He has not abandoned us in our trials. He is the One who is empowering us to hold up under the pressure we are feeling. He is the same God who has placed all there is that is good in our lives, and there is much more to come that we have not yet begun to imagine. We can be strengthened in those truths and express our feelings of thankfulness knowing the role He plays in our daily lives.

Most recently I kept reminding myself that God was the source of every good thing in my life. He gave me a saving relationship with Him through Jesus Christ. He blessed me with a wonderful family. He opened the door for me to have a means of income through my business. He gave me the health and ability to do the work associated with that business. Without God, I would have nothing. My life would be meaningless and empty. I would not even have breath in my body.

When I realized that I was solely dependent upon my God, joy emerged. The pressure of uncertainty turned to confidence in the One who has provided all else. With that confidence came joy. I had no need to concern myself with any task other than giving God praise for what He was going to do. How He would fix the problem was irrelevant and clearly none of my business. His expectation for me was to trust Him and walk in the strength of the joy that accompanies knowing who He is and who I am in Him.

Joy produces growth. I love ice cream. Like every young couple starting out in life, finances were a challenge for my wife and me. I oversaw the checkbook. At times my wife would indicate trepidation about our financial situation. I assured her that as long as we had ice cream in the freezer, there was nothing to worry about. When I was a kid, I was only acquainted with one flavor of ice cream. My world expanded greatly when I learned that there were other flavors besides vanilla. I wanted to explore the depths of this knowledge to its fullest. I am sixty-one years old, and while I may have my favorite, I am never opposed to experiencing something new and exciting when it comes to ice cream.

The more we delve into the joy of the Lord, the more we desire to experience a deeper understanding of who God is. Joy is like the feeling we had when we first fell in love with our spouse. It is like the adrenaline rush we experienced on that rope swing at our old swimming hole the moment we gained enough courage to give it a try. It is a compelling force that drives us forward. It makes us want more of the same but with an added twist that never leaves us bored. There is no end to the joy of the Lord. It is everlasting and inexhaustible. It has only one deterrent. That deterrent is us. The only force that can kill our joy is our willingness to allow it to occur.

> THERE IS NO END TO THE JOY OF THE LORD. IT IS EVERLASTING AND INEXHAUSTIBLE.

If we choose to ignore the joy that is always available, we choose to walk in the flesh. The flesh carries with it nothing but doubt and shame and uncertainty. It draws attention to our failures and our limitations rather than God's acceptance and empowerment. In Nehemiah chapter 8, there is a story which I call the "first revival" ever recorded in Scripture. Many of the Jews had been allowed to return from captivity in Babylon to rebuild the city of Jerusalem. They had managed to rebuild the walls of the city. Nehemiah and Ezra brought the people together to reacquaint them with the Word of God that had been given to them many years prior. As the people heard the law, their hearts sank. They realized how far they had fallen. They were smitten with guilt and shame. The leaders of Israel encouraged them that day to lift up their hands! They were told to celebrate and to be glad. This was not a time to grieve over the past. It was a time to rejoice in the future. They were encouraged with the words "The joy of the Lord is your strength" (Nehemiah 8:10).

The Jewish people were to forget the past failures and see themselves in a new light. They were to look to the future with hope and encouragement because it was obvious that God was a God of mercy, forgiveness, and redemption. Israel was through paying for its mistakes. It had now embarked on a new journey of prosperity and peace because the people were once again walking in the ways of the Lord. We may face difficulties as a result of our own past mistakes, but even then, we can still find joy for the taking. God meets us right where we are. He never changes. He is still working on our behalf. He will see us through whatever we must endure until the trial is passed. Joy is always a possibility.

If you want more joy, seek a more intimate relationship with Christ. Joy is a fruit of the Holy Spirit. If you plant a field of tomato plants, you may need to have a good recipe for catsup because you will soon have a lot of fruit to work with. Joy will be unavoidable if you cultivate a vibrant ongoing relationship with the Lord. Everything connected with God produces joy. If you spend time reading and studying the Word of God you will experience joy. If you devote "face time" each day talking to God in prayer, you will experience joy. If you seek to be used of the Lord in some type of service ministering to the needs of others, you will be overtaken with joy. Someone once said that *JOY* stands for *Jesus, Others, and You.* When we align our priorities with God's agenda, we will see a constant flow of joy in our lives.

My wife and I pastored a church in the small town of Noel Missouri. Not long after we came there a home missionary who I later became best friends with helped our church reach out to our community. He taught us how to share Jesus with others. He equipped us with resources we had no means to pay for. He organized our efforts so that in a few hours, our small body of Christ was able to knock on every door in our community of about two thousand people.

That morning, before we left the place, it was quiet and tense. Anxiety was obvious. Many of the folks had never knocked on someone's door, prayed with a stranger, or shared the Gospel. We prayed for each one to have boldness and success and then we broke up into small teams. Lunch was provided at the church for the workers as they returned back from their morning of ministry. The place was electric. It sounded like a bunch of kids returning from the circus. Story after story was shared about how God used them to encourage someone or found a need they could meet in some way. There was laughing and loud camaraderie. More than anything there was joy. Joy was abounding. It was like someone had opened up a fire hydrant full of the stuff and it was spraying everywhere.

I learned something from that experience. I had attended church for many years and often wondered why so many who come each week seem so unhappy about being there. There are always those who are the first to complain or judge. Nothing seems to satisfy them. I would often wonder what was lacking in their lives. The answer was joy. Joy does not automatically come from church attendance or even tithing. It is not a natural byproduct of singing in the choir or leading a small group. Joy can be associated with all those things if they are done out of a heart for God. However, we will not experience joy by merely doing what we think is required. We must do what we do because we love God and we want to do His will.

The Bible declared in Hebrews 12:2 that we should look to Jesus, the author, and finisher of our faith, who for the joy that was set before Him endured the cross. Christ paid the ultimate price on our behalf because of the joy of being obedient to the Father and the privilege of providing us a means of salvation. He endured the greatest trial known to mankind, and he did so with joy. He was our example. Thankfully God will never require us to experience what Christ did. However, Jesus did say that we would experience persecution and suffering and affliction. He set the bar high but showed us how a man filled with the Holy Spirit could endure the utmost if needed. And He did it with joy.

Perhaps you are currently experiencing a great trial. Lift up your head. Take note of who you are and who God is. Forgive and be forgiven. Take control of your thoughts. Stop considering those things which produce anxiety and depression. Think on those things that are praiseworthy. Count your many blessings. Practice the attitude of gratitude and give thanks for what God has done and what He is going to do. Look beyond yourself and see what you can do to aid someone who is in greater need. Remember that our Lord has already endured the utmost in order to enable us to be overcomers. Practice prayer and find strength in the joy that communion with God brings. Let the Word of God which contains so many stories of victorious Saints paint a picture of hope. Most of all, never forget that the *JOY OF THE LORD IS YOUR STRENGTH!*

CHAPTER 11

MATURITY

*Maturity enables us to understand
the purpose of the trial.*

I spent several years at war with my father. From age fifteen, I was
in full-blown rebellion to any and every type of authority, but
especially my dad's. I grew up in the home of a strict preacher
with more rules than I could count. I wanted nothing to do with
God, church, or parental authority. Our conflict was ongoing and
never ceasing. Yet through it all, my dad never stopped loving me
or trying to help me. I called him every name in the book, and
we pushed and shoved each other with our noses inches apart. I
can still feel the spit landing on my face from one of our many
screaming matches. The funny thing is that he was always right. I
could never learn from my mistakes.

Many of the things my father warned me about sounded
ludicrous at the time he said them. One afternoon I burst into the
house and immediately began searching through the beaded purse

where my mother stored important documents. I had decided that it was in my best interest to put my car up as collateral to a drug dealer in order to make a profit. I was sure that within a couple of days I could sell the dope, get the car back, and pad my pockets in the process.

"You are going to lose your car, son," my dad said without even knowing the details. I thought about how stupid he was to the ways of the streets. He had no understanding regarding the number of connections a "kingpin" drug dealer like me had. He clearly had not done the math. He was unaware of the amount of money a person could make given the right set of circumstances. After all, he was a fifty-something preacher with a sixth-grade education.

My plan went just as expected. I gave the dealer my car and got the goods. In two days, I had cut it, sold it and was back at his front door with cash in hand ready to retrieve my like-new 1975 Chevy Caprice. However, instead of getting my car keys placed back in my hand I was met with a shotgun in my face. The guy looked at me and laughed. "Did you really think I was going to give you your car back after you signed the title over to me?" he asked. "You must be more stupid than you look" he added. "Now get off my porch, or I am going to blow you off of it."

My dad was right, again. He was always right. Looking back over my life I cannot recall one occasion when my father told me something that did not come to pass. How did he know all that stuff? He did not have to be acquainted with all the details of my life to see the direction I was headed. I can remember him telling me that I was going to end up in prison. In fact, I thought about that quite a bit during the fourteen-plus months I sat in a Texas penitentiary. He told me God had a calling on my life. I laughed at him and called him crazy. But after thirty-two years in the ministry, I must admit he had some insight I wasn't willing to acknowledge.

My dad was not a psychic. He wasn't a genius either. He was mature. Maturity gives a person the ability to see the big picture. Sometimes the way things look is not the way things are. Take Abraham for example. Here was an old man who had waited decades to have a biological son with his wife who was way past her prime. Finally, after years of waiting and only by means of the miraculous, Isaac is born. Then the story really gets crazy.

> MATURITY GIVES A PERSON THE ABILITY TO SEE THE BIG PICTURE. SOMETIMES THE WAY THINGS LOOK IS NOT THE WAY THINGS ARE.

God speaks to Abraham and tells him to take his only son that he waited so long to have and kill him on the top of a mountain. Everything associated with this command screamed foul. After all, wasn't it God who gave him the son? Wasn't it God who said it would be through this child that Abraham's name and nation would flourish? What kind of craziness was this?

The Bible says that Abraham got up early in the morning and promptly headed out for the mountain of death. He wasted no time. He took his son and prepared the boy for slaughter just as he would a lamb or an ox. He took his knife out of his belt and raised it for the killing blow. At the last second, God stopped Abraham and praises him for his faith. It wasn't mere faith that enabled Abraham to pass the test. It was maturity. Abraham's maturity had enabled him to see past the mountain he climbed that morning and look towards what lay on the other side. He even told the men that came with him that he and the boy would return after worshipping God. He had no doubt that God had a plan. He just didn't know all the details.

Faith pushed Abraham out of the comfort zone of his homeland many years prior. Faith had encouraged Abraham to hang tough when things got hard and he made some poor choices. Faith even produced a child when it appeared to be an impossible task. But faith alone did not enable this man of God to place his son on an altar of sacrifice with every intention of slitting his throat. That, my friend, was maturity. Abraham had reached a place of maturity in his walk with God. He knew that even though what was being asked sounded ridiculous, it would not thwart God's plan. The situation he was facing did not change the big picture. It only enabled him to experience one more supernatural encounter with God and reaffirmed that God's plan is always best. Everything God had promised him prior to that moment became even more of a reality.

Our heavenly Father always knows how things are going to turn out. Just like my dad, He sees the pitfalls ahead and our propensity to fall prey to them. When our faith reaches the point of maturity that it is succinct with God's ultimate plan, we walk in a realm of trust that is like no other. We understand that the trial we face has purpose. We embrace it as such. I am not suggesting that we be the first to volunteer to be put through God's wringer. I am suggesting that when we find ourselves being severely pressed that we should recognize the value in the process.

God doesn't operate on our level. Too often we try to deal with life's problems without the maturity to understand the ultimate goal. James said in James 1:2-4 that we should rejoice when we face trials because they are a means of making us complete and lacking nothing. I have sat through many prayer requests being uttered in a church service. People request prayer for all sorts of things. If they run out of needs of their own, there are always the starving children in third world countries or world peace to consider. However, in light of James' exhortation, you would think that someone would ask God to send them a hard trial so that their spiritual growth process would be expedited. Yet I have yet to see anyone rise to their feet during one of those prayer services and say, "Pastor, would you pray that God will send me a good ole trial so I can grow in the Lord?" It hasn't happened yet, and it probably never will. Nobody wants a trial. You would be crazy if you did.

James did not suggest that we ask for a severe struggle to come our way. He said to rejoice in the fact that when it does occur we are sure to become more mature. An elderly lady was going through a severe time of difficulty in her life. Everything that could go wrong pretty much had gone wrong. A well-meaning youth pastor tried to encourage her one Sunday morning by telling her that he was praying for her. She looked at him and smiled.

"What exactly are you praying for. young man?" she asked.

"Well... I am praying that your husband will get a job, that your financial situation will increase, that your health will improve, and that your daughter will come to know Christ and stop living so rebelliously" he responded.

"I appreciate that," she said. "But will you please just pray that I will learn whatever lesson the Lord is trying to teach me through all of this?" she asked. That is the definition of maturity

> MATURITY IS THE ABILITY TO LOOK BEYOND THE IMMEDIATE AND SEE THE DIVINE PURPOSE.

in the midst of a trial. Maturity is the ability to look beyond the immediate and see the divine purpose.

Things are rarely as they appear when it comes to the way God interacts with us. Most people come to the Lord out of inspiration or desperation. In my case, it was the latter. From the outside looking in, my life looked hopeless. I had overdosed on one occasion and attempted suicide on another. I had severed myself from every good person who genuinely cared about my welfare. From all points of view, it seemed certain that if I did not end up in prison, I would most likely end up dead. My dad had prayed for me for thirteen years. One day, he was lying on his face before God and told God that he had prayed all the prayers he could utter, and like Abraham, he was placing me on the altar and in the hands of the Father. God spoke to my dad and said, "What Abraham put on the altar he did not lose."

I gave my heart to Christ only a couple of weeks later. What appeared to be a hopeless, futile effort on Dad's part was an act of mature faith. He understood that regardless of how far I had run, I could not escape the heart and hand of the One who gave me that life to begin with.

Sometimes the most mature thing we can do is surrender. We must be willing to take our hands off of what God is trying to accomplish. We must realize that He is always the One with the master plan. God never does

> SOMETIMES THE MOST MATURE THING WE CAN DO IS SURRENDER.

anything that does not contribute to the blueprints of our lives. He uses people and circumstances and tragedies to His benefit. Satan has nothing available in his arsenal of weapons formed against us that God will not use to help us to mature in Christ. When things happen that seem to have absolutely no purpose, there is still good that can come out of it. We have seen it occur time and again when people's lives are rocked with tragedy or a mass shooting or some other horrific event. After the dust settles a movement starts, or a ministry is launched. Perhaps legislation is introduced, or other people are motivated to pick up the torch and carry the banner.

Recently my wife began following the story of a young teenage boy who was a Christian and avid pro-life advocate. He was suddenly stricken with terminal cancer. In the face of his life being taken at such a young age, his story became widely published on social media. He saw the opportunity to use his sickness as a platform to promote right choices regarding the lives of unborn children. He wrote a compelling and moving letter to the members of his generation regarding their responsibility to stand up for the cause of righteousness. It was one of the most powerful documents I had ever read. God allowed that letter to gain notoriety and it was printed on the front page of a newspaper in London, England. That is a long way from Waco, Texas where it was penned. He spent his last waking hours worshipping God and speaking the Word of the Lord. The level of maturity he exhibited rivals that of David Brainerd or Jim Elliott. He understood that being spent for the cause of Christ was the ultimate privilege.

We witnessed that same type of mature faith in the manner in which Rachel Scott died along with thirteen others at the Columbine High School shooting. When being asked by a crazed shooter if she believed in God and knowing that an affirmative answer would result in being executed, she chose not to deny her Lord. Her funeral drew the most viewers in the history of television in 1999. More than JFK. Her story still continues to inspire young believers worldwide to not be ashamed of their faith in Christ.

Maturity produces a faith that understands that there are no limits on how God can use a trial to benefit the Kingdom. There are no boundaries or rules that prohibit Christ from birthing glory from the seed of evil. Stephen was the first martyr in Christendom. His death opened the floodgates of persecution against the early church. As a result, believers ran for their lives, and as they ran, they preached. They told others about the Gospel because the Good News was alive in their hearts. Later, the apostles and missionaries came as well, and the ground was fertile for planting. It should not have been a surprise when Phillip experienced such great success in Samaria. A short while previous an outcast woman sat on the side of a well and received the message of hope from the Messiah Himself. It all worked together for good. That is the truth that mature faith rests on.

> **THERE ARE NO BOUNDARIES OR RULES THAT PROHIBIT CHRIST FROM BIRTHING GLORY FROM THE SEED OF EVIL.**

Marty was an awesome guy. You would not have thought it merely be looking at him or reading his resume. He was quiet, mild-mannered, and soft-spoken. His life consisted of pretty much the same thing every week. He attended church, and he went to work. He was employed at the local chicken plant and worked in the freezer. He walked to work on occasion in the summer months wearing gear fit for the artic. I learned that many in town referred to him as the "chicken man." When he had transportation, it was usually an old car or truck that was on its last leg.

Marty attended my church and eventually lived right across the street from me. He had two teenage sons that were fairly rowdy. I learned that Marty's wife left him for a methamphetamine cook when they were very young. He raised the boys all by himself. He was unwilling and unable to get a divorce because he always had hopes she would come back. He also had no idea where she was. It seemed like Marty's life was pretty much stuck on hold. Church was a big deal to Marty. He never missed. He loved to sing the old hymns and would throw his head back and let it fly. He had a great baritone voice.

One day we noticed Marty sitting in a different spot than usual. He had moved closer to our church secretary who was a single mom with a young son. Love had sparked. Marty and Candace were married, and it was not long before they had a beautiful little girl that they named Hannah. It was awesome to see two people whose lives had seemed so stifled suddenly began to burst forth like the flowers of spring.

Then something horrible happened. Marty began having some physical difficulties and was diagnosed with advanced pancreatic cancer. The doctors did what they do, but it was pretty obvious that they were not the answer. If Marty was to survive, it would take a miracle from God. Fortunately, Marty attended a church where divine healing was often preached. Our small body of Christ joined together like a bunch of Holy Spirit Power Rangers. There was enough faith in our prayers to move a hundred mountains much less to cure one case of cancer. There was not one morning I was not crying out to God in intercession for my friend and brother in Christ to be healed.

I woke up in the middle of the night with a voice ringing in my ear that Marty was gone. It had to be the Lord because no one else was awake. Seconds later the phone rang to confirm the message I had just received. I was crushed. How could I ever again tell anyone that God heals the sick? How could I not feel like a hypocrite or charlatan if I ever again muttered a word about how we serve a God of miracles who told us to just ask and it would happen? How could I even find the strength to continue to preach at all? My faith was shaken to its very core.

Even worse than that, I was angry. I was very angry. Marty was my friend. I spent twelve days rooming with him on a mission trip to El Salvador. He came to my aid once at a time when I felt no one else could possibly understand what I was going through. I was angry, and that anger was slowly eating away at the calling that God had placed on my life. How could God not honor my faith and that of the church body? Did He even do this kind of thing anymore? Was this some sick joke He played on weak-minded believers who were gullible enough to believe in the supernatural?

The anger ended one Sunday at an altar of prayer. I had scheduled a guest speaker who had preached better than I was capable of at that moment. I found myself standing off to the side of the church, and it was like God decided to have a showdown and suddenly it was high noon. I was trying to pray which was difficult when you were mad at the One you were praying to.

Then I unmistakably heard the Lord speak to me. "You're mad, aren't you? You are angry because your friend died," He said.

"Yes!" I answered. It felt like my spirit was shouting from within me. "Yes, I'm mad at you because you DID take my friend from me" I replied.

Then the Lord said these words, "For God so loved the world that He gave His only begotten Son that whosoever believeth Him SHALL NOT PERISH...SHALL NOT PERISH...SHALL NOT PERISH...Your friend is not dead," God said. "He is more alive than he has ever been. You are angry at me for something I did not do."

My heart melted, and I fell at His feet asking for forgiveness. I had been trying to hold God accountable for something that did not even occur. Yes, Marty was gone, but he was not dead. He was and is alive evermore. My faith grew that day. I became more mature as I began to better understand the eternal realm and plans of God. Maturity helps us to see past that mountain of death and fully drink in the sunrise that is occurring on the other side.

> MATURITY HELPS US TO SEE PAST THAT MOUNTAIN OF DEATH AND FULLY DRINK IN THE SUNRISE THAT IS OCCURRING ON THE OTHER SIDE.

Alex was an ex-policeman who was built for the job. His large frame was enough to put a scare into most would-be lawbreakers. However, lung cancer slowly transformed this mountain of a man into merely a shadow of what he once was. I came to know Alex by what I thought was happenstance. He operated a used furniture store next to an outreach center we had established in our town. Although I was frequently doing business at his store, our relationship was pretty rocky. His dad was an ex-preacher who failed to live up to his calling which tainted his view of me. I, on the other hand, have never had fond affection for policemen considering my past scrapes with the law.

It was God's divine plan working in both our lives. After Alex was diagnosed with terminal cancer, he and his entire family eventually gave their hearts to Christ at our church. As the end drew near for Alex, my heart became heavier. One day I went to his house. The disease had reached a point that he could no longer attend church. I brought with me a small communion set and just he and I partook of The Lord's Supper for what I expected to be the last time. I became emotional and began to weep at the thought of losing someone I had grown to love.

Mature faith began to emerge. Alex looked at me and smiled. "Aren't you my pastor?" he asked.

"Yes. Of course, I am," I answered. I was a bit puzzled at such a question at a time like that.

"Isn't it your job to help me get to heaven?" he asked.

"Well...yes," I replied.

"Then why are you crying? You should be happy because I will soon be there," he said. Mature faith enabled Alex to look beyond the funeral and the potato salad that often follows and see the eternal reward that awaited him. He did so not with fear or sadness but with joy and expectancy.

Time is not an important element when it comes to maturity in the spiritual realm. One can grow rapidly given the right set of circumstances. Those circumstances usually involve some amount of suffering. Rarely do we obtain the kind of faith I am attempting to describe without a trial. Too often we are focused on God only when it suits our fancies or fits into our busy schedules. That focus becomes more intense when life is at risk. We tend to gain a new level of spiritual understanding when we discover that the things which we often hold so dear are fragile. Nothing is unshakable except for God and that which is directly related to Him. That is why faith is so important. It withstands the greatest of threats and can fend

TIME IS NOT AN IMPORTANT ELEMENT WHEN IT COMES TO MATURITY IN THE SPIRITUAL REALM. ONE CAN GROW RAPIDLY GIVEN THE RIGHT SET OF CIRCUMSTANCES.

off the most intense attacks. Our increasing awareness increased our spiritual maturity. The more confident we are in our faith, the more mature we are in Christ.

We all recall those times when we stood against the wall, and our mom or dad measured our height. Each time we went through the ritual a new mark was added. We could easily stand back and gaze at the progress we had made. It would be great if that was a means of identifying our spiritual growth. It is not. In order to see the development that has occurred, we must be placed in positions in which we are forced to exhibit our maturity. Our response to trials is as much a gauge of growth as those pencil marks on the wall.

My son-in-law came to know the Lord as a young child but like most of us did not begin a serious faith walk until adulthood. I have watched him spiritually mature at a rapid rate. That growth did not occur without challenges. He recently related a series of events that he identified as a catalyst for his spiritual maturity.

He and my daughter had just bought a home, and it soon became apparent that there was more outgo than income in their finances. He is the type of person that likes to plan ahead. He doesn't like surprises. His focus is always on making sure that his family is secure. He takes that job very seriously. I very much appreciate that my daughter and grandsons are of the utmost importance to him. However, life has a way of wrenching that control out of our hands periodically. That is when the opportunity for growth and maturity usually occur.

Dustin knew that he needed an increase in his paycheck if they were going to survive. He asked his boss for a raise that he considered timely and well deserved. The answer did not come right away. In fact, it did not seem that it would come at all. He continued to work hard in an effort to live up to the biblical principle of honoring those in authority over you. He has always had a great work ethic. He did not allow the lack of response to hinder the amount of effort his boss had come to expect. Instead, he identified whatever changes he saw that he could personally make to alleviate the situation. He decided to sell his truck he loved so dearly and downsize a bit. In the process, he was able to get a larger vehicle more appropriate for the size of his family. His savings was still depleting, however.

Dustin remained hopeful and prayed daily that God would somehow make a way of escape. On the days that were most difficult, he prayed even harder. When they would see a glimmer of hope, such as a slight increase in his wife's pay, another expense would pop up which seemed to cancel out the progress. At one point in the process, my daughter lost her job, which truly threatened to sink their little ship. They did not give up hope. He continued to trust the Lord that an answer was on the way. His wife soon got another job but the much-needed raise he had asked for almost 10 months prior seemed just as elusive as ever.

One day Dustin picked up his check and saw that there was a noticeable increase. In fact, it was exactly the amount he had asked for! Full of joy and gratitude he reached out to his employer to express his thankfulness for the raise he thought had finally arrived. That joy quickly diminished when he learned that it was not a regular increase in pay but merely a one-time bonus due to some extra income the company had received. He was crushed.

He wanted to give up. He instead reached down inside of himself and anchored his hope to the foundation of his faith. He continued to pray and give God thanks for a solution to their problem. The answer came only two days later. The misunderstanding about his paycheck actually brought the subject of the raise to his employer's attention. A meeting was scheduled with his boss, and he received that much-needed increase. Dustin would later look back on the ordeal and acknowledge that it was all for his good. His faith matured. A mature believer does not throw in the towel. A mature believer gets off the mat and faces each round with stability and endurance.

I was always told that how we go through a test determines whether we will take it again. The children of Israel were the best at failing tests. Faced with a lack of food or water, they immediately complained or doubted God's goodness. Their memories were short even after witnessing some of the greatest miracles ever recorded. A trial will always pass. A test will undoubtedly end at some point. The issue is how we responded during the course of it all. Maturity produces praise and gratitude rather than moans and groans. Mature faith does not produce complaints. It does not throw pity parties. Mature faith never doubts the goodness of God. Mature faith looks for the purpose and not the solution.

We cannot help but grow if we remain connected to Christ. He is the giver of life. Every believer grows at some pace. However, the more we are forced to exercise the faith we are developing, the quicker we mature. The faster we mature, the stronger we become. Similarly, as we mature, we develop immunity to the enemy's attacks. We become like the palm tree whose taproot extends into the ground as far as the tree extends upward.

MATURITY PRODUCES PRAISE AND GRATITUDE RATHER THAN MOANS AND GROANS. MATURE FAITH DOES NOT PRODUCE COMPLAINTS. IT DOES NOT THROW PITY PARTIES. MATURE FAITH NEVER DOUBTS THE GOODNESS OF GOD. MATURE FAITH LOOKS FOR THE PURPOSE AND NOT THE SOLUTION.

The winds of life assail against it, and all it does is bend. It bends, but it does not break. It is so well rooted and grounded that the fiercest hurricane is unable to bring it down.

Maturity has the same effect. We may face the storm and feel the wind, but we only bend. We will not break. We know many storms have come and gone in the past. We are also aware of the life-giving connection to God that will never allow us to fall. Each time we are tested we only become stronger. Our maturity in Christ assures us that the sun will always shine again. We are confident that each trial makes us more whole and complete and unstoppable. Our strength is not in our ability but in our awareness of the new day that is always dawning on the other side of the mountain we are climbing.

CHAPTER 12

EXPECTANCY

Expect the answer to be on the way.

The pregnant woman was wheeled into the hospital elevator. The nurse pushed the button marked 10. The delivery room was already prepared for her arrival. She was moments away from giving birth. Suddenly the elevator came to a screeching halt as it stalled in between two floors. The lady looked up at the nurse with panic in her eyes. It was obvious they would not make it to their destination in time.

The RN smiled and said "Don't feel bad. Last year a lady had her baby on the front lawn."

"I know," said the expectant mom, "that was me!"

Some things are going to happen regardless of opposition. They are inevitable. The ocean tide will come in and go out four times a day. The sun will rise and set every twenty-four hours.

What goes up will eventually come down thanks to the pull of gravity on the earth's surface. There will always be evil in the world. Every Christian is going to experience some hard times. It's just the way things are.

Along with many of the negatives that we can bank on during our time on the planet, we also have some promises that are just as definite. Jesus told his disciples that in this world we would have trouble. However, He also said that we should cheer up because He has overcome the world (John 16:33).

David wrote in Psalms 34:19, "Many are the afflictions of the righteous but the Lord delivereth him out of them all." A victorious outcome in every situation is guaranteed to all Christians. It may not be the result we would have orchestrated. However, it will be the result that God has determined, and it will serve to bring Him glory.

> A VICTORIOUS OUTCOME IN EVERY SITUATION IS GUARANTEED TO ALL CHRISTIANS. IT MAY NOT BE THE RESULT WE WOULD HAVE ORCHESTRATED. HOWEVER, IT WILL BE THE RESULT THAT GOD HAS DETERMINED, AND IT WILL SERVE TO BRING HIM GLORY.

I love what is often referred to as the "faith chapter" in the book of Hebrews. It begins by listing all the heroes of faith. Men like Abraham and Moses and Noah are at the top of the list. But possibly more important are the unnamed folks at the bottom of the list. It describes people who endured severe trials such as mock trials, false imprisonment, extreme torture, and martyrdom. They are heralded with as much acclaim as those who subdued kingdoms and saw the dead raised to life. The reward that they received is described by the writer of the book as them obtaining a good report by God. That is the ultimate form of acclaim.

I had a Bible college instructor who often spoke of the degree that we were all striving to obtain through our hard work and diligence. We expected that it would result in a day when we would be clothed in a cap and gown, walk across the stage, and be handed a diploma by the president of the college. Our elderly instructor told us of a much higher degree that we should endeavor to achieve. He referred to it as the *A.U.G. degree*. We looked puzzled when he first uttered those words. Then he read the exhortation Paul wrote to Timothy in 2 Timothy 2:15 which said that we should "study to show ourselves approved unto God." A.U.G. stood for approved unto God.

In order to obtain that goal, we need to know what God expects from us. Of all the choices, the one that stands out most is to trust God. If we trust God, everything else is merely icing on the cake. It is the secret to obtaining eternal life. It is the key to victorious Christian living. It is the catalyst to effective ministry. It is the means by which we come to understand the Word of God as it was meant to be understood. It is the foundation and building blocks to overcoming faith. Those folks at the end of that chapter in Hebrews all had one thing in common. They trusted God. As a result, they knew what to expect.

Expectancy is not some flaky hope-so term. Expectancy means that everything inside of us has bought into the idea that something is going to happen. We may not know the details, but we can be assured of the final outcome. We might not know the time frame, but we know it is inevitable. We serve a God who

EXPECTANCY IS NOT SOME FLAKY HOPE-SO TERM. EXPECTANCY MEANS THAT EVERYTHING INSIDE OF US HAS BOUGHT INTO THE IDEA THAT SOMETHING IS GOING TO HAPPEN.

never fails. He is not like a man who lies or disappoints. He is not limited in His ability. He is never in a quandary as to what needs to be done next. He is all-powerful, all-knowing, and ever-present. We should live our lives in a constant state of expectancy. There is never a moment in our existence in which God is not in the process of doing something in our lives. He never does anything that is not meant to bring Him glory or thwart the enemy of our souls.

So what does it look like to live our lives with expectant faith? My father-in-law would describe it as having a little man inside of you who is constantly doing backflips. In other words, there is an ever-present sense of excitement. Every day God is doing something extraordinary. Some days it becomes more obvious than other days. The fun part is that we never know what day it is that He is planning on revealing a part of Himself or His plan for our lives that we haven't already seen.

I rarely go to the mailbox that I don't wonder if there is a bit of good news awaiting me. It is easy for me to imagine a future that far exceeds my present. I know what God is capable of. I also believe that He is just as likely to include me in some grand scheme as not. What I might not experience is not worth considering. That's no fun. Conjuring up an ill-fated future in my mind is unprofitable. It defies what I believe about God. I had much rather consider the magnificent possibilities associated with a God who is limitless and loves me like His own Son. That produces expectant faith.

If the devil has one main tool he uses more than any other, it has to be discouragement. He knows that discouragement causes doubt, so in the midst of a trial, he does his best to paint the most dismal picture possible about the outcome. It is impossible to express overcoming faith out of a heart of discouragement. It causes us to look at the present rather than the future. We begin to take inventory of the resources that are specific to us instead of the riches of Christ. We begin to lean on our strength rather than the power of God. And possibly worst of all, we take it upon ourselves to define our future rather than what God's Word declares.

It would have been easy for me to predict a dismal outcome during my most recent trial. I could have perceived a financial disaster in the making. Satan wanted me to buy into the idea that the business I spent the last thirteen years building was doomed to fall in a matter of weeks. He urged me to consider what it would be like for my wife to lose her dream house and be forced to move. He would remind me how the reputation I had established in the therapeutic community would be destroyed. He especially wanted me to remember that I am over 60 years old and not in a position to start over.

While I cannot say that those thoughts did not cross my mind, I can say that I did not allow them to set up shop in my head. I got up every morning and read the Good News of the Gospel. I filled my day with audio sermons preached by men who believed that nothing was too hard for God. My faith grew more than ever. As my faith grew, so did my level of expectancy. It was contagious. It spread to my wife as well. We would sit and talk about how God is going to fix our problem and what means

AS MY FAITH GREW, SO DID MY LEVEL OF EXPECTANCY.

He might use. Even though the solution did not look exactly like what we imagined, we had a great time thinking about it. We were more and more encouraged as the deadline grew closer. We knew that God was never late and He never failed, so our excitement built as time ran out. He did just as we expected.

Expectant faith produces action. There is a reason why many refer to our Christian experience as a walk of faith. *Faith that does not eventually produce movement is useless.* Expectancy is moving forward on what we know rather than what we see. It may sound risky, but it is essential. Expectancy is like the foot on the gas pedal

> EXPECTANT FAITH
> PRODUCES ACTION.
> THERE IS A REASON WHY
> MANY REFER TO OUR
> CHRISTIAN EXPERIENCE
> AS A WALK OF FAITH.
> FAITH THAT DOES NOT
> EVENTUALLY PRODUCE
> MOVEMENT IS USELESS.

that drives us further down the road towards the answer we so desperately seek.

I live in a dream house. It is not elaborate or expensive, but it was birthed from a desire that my wife had in her heart from the time she was a teenager. She drew the floor plan on a piece of paper and held onto it for over thirty years before it became a reality. Our first twenty years of marriage were financially challenging. I mostly worked as a self-employed garage door installer. It paid the bills but not much more. Things improved after I went back to college and became a professional counselor. However, the concept of building a house was foreign to us. She began to visualize what it would feel like to have our own home situated in a place surrounded by trees. Her dream became a reality but not before a process.

My wife and my daughter drove around our area and happened upon forty acres of thick woods. We made the purchase. Weekends were often spent with a newly purchased chain saw and weedeater as we forged a path to the middle of the property where she could visualize us one day residing. Little by little the dream became a reality. I learned that once the process begins, it becomes easier to conceive the end result. Expectancy grew as we walked through this new experience. I could imagine what it might feel like to enjoy the pleasure of making her dream come true. That day of course came, and it met our every expectation.

I learned that once we chart a path toward an end result and begin the process, expectancy is a natural occurrence. Facing trials is much the same way. We can sit and dream, or we can start hacking away at the obstacles that stand in our paths to victory. As we begin the walk forward, our hearts become filled with the excitement of seeing the conclusion We imagine what it will be like when it is all over and we have reached our goals. With each day our level of expectancy increases and with it the determination to complete.

Expectancy should be a way of life. Jesus told His disciples to expect miracles. He told them to expect trouble. He told them to expect results. He told them to expect His return. He told them to expect a reward. For us to convince ourselves that things are always going to remain the same is foolish. We are going to encounter some challenges in the form of trials. We are also going to suffer a bit. Along with the trials we should also expect to see God's hand in ways that we have yet to experience. We should expect to grow in our faith and knowledge. Our love for God and

> EXPECTANCY SHOULD BE A WAY OF LIFE. JESUS TOLD HIS DISCIPLES TO EXPECT MIRACLES.

others should increase. We should expect that good is going to emerge from the ashes of trouble.

None of this expectation should be based on mere positive thinking. I often hear so-called preachers feed their listeners the lie that everything will be fine if they will merely think good thoughts. They tell us to take note of the sun shining or the birds singing and refocus our minds onto happy reflections. The Bible does encourage us to monitor our thought life. That is true. However, if positive thinking is all that is required to live a happy and fulfilled life there would be no need for Christ or the Holy Spirit. The rankest of sinners could live as fulfilled a life as the strongest believer.

Expectant faith is based on knowledge of God rooted in a relationship with Christ. I can rise above the clouds of doubt because I know Jesus intimately. I am convinced He is at work in my life regardless of the circumstances that may be present. I am also convinced that those circumstances will come to a desired end because that is how God operates. If my spirit is lifted up by listening to the birds singing in the morning, it is because I am reminded of who created them and sustains them. It is not because I train myself to somehow dissociate from my problems.

EXPECTANT FAITH IS BASED ON KNOWLEDGE OF GOD ROOTED IN A RELATIONSHIP WITH CHRIST.

Sometimes God does the unexpected just so that we will learn to expect that as well. You may need to read that sentence a couple of times before it may sink in. Yes, God wants us to expect the unexpected. It sounds impossible, but it actually frees us up to

> SOMETIMES GOD DOES THE UNEXPECTED JUST SO THAT WE WILL LEARN TO EXPECT THAT AS WELL.

truly operate in a realm of the Spirit that transcends human limitations. There have been times when God has purposely shown up and shown out in ways that blew my mind. It was as if He just wanted to have some fun and remind me that He can do whatever He chooses however He chooses. Sometimes it happens right out of the blue when everything seems to be going smoothly. He doesn't need a dilemma to reveal Himself to us.

Often, He imparts little nuggets of information to us for later use. How many times has God shown up in your life unexpectedly? Perhaps nothing was wrong, and life seemed to be going well and suddenly out of nowhere – BAM – a supernatural event occurred. God orchestrates divine encounters and drops blessings out of the sky like unexpected summer rain. He does this to give us something to remember when times are difficult. It is a reference point that leads us back to the reality that He is limitless.

I was dressed for church one Sunday morning and turned on the TV to kill a little time before I had to leave. I would often try to catch a snippet of preaching from one of the few TV evangelists I found credible. However, when the program appeared, it was someone I had never seen before, and as you might guess, he was talking about money. I would have immediately turned the channel except that he seemed sincere. I only watched for a little while, but during that time the minister spoke of a *faith seed*. He said an amount of money too small to be considered a harvest must undoubtedly be a seed. He used a thousand dollars as an example. While one thousand dollars is certainly a bit of change, it is certainly not a harvest because it would not go far in liquidating debt or sending your child to college. He proclaimed that if it is not a harvest, then it must be a seed. I turned off Mike Murdock and headed to church.

The thought lingered in my mind. I could not think of a time when I had the means to give God an offering of that size. I prayed aloud to God and said, "Lord, I wish I could give you a thousand dollars." That day our small church contained the same faithful few as normal. They were not wealthy people, but most were very consistent in their giving. As I prepared to receive the offering, I told them what I had heard that morning on the television. I challenged them to be sensitive to the Holy Spirit and to give as He would lead them.

My salary was determined by a certain percentage of the offerings received each Sunday. It would vary each week usually from $200-$400. As I was leaving the church that morning, I took note of the amount of the offering that had been given. I was astounded beyond belief. My part alone was going to amount to around $1,800! Immediately I knew that God was up to something and that most of that money was not meant for me personally.

Approximately eighteen people were in attendance for the Sunday evening service. As we were having a time of prayer after the sermon, I felt led to personally pray for a young couple. As I was praying for them, I sensed they were struggling financially and asked God to intervene. He spoke to me in my spirit and said, "You begin the process." Now I knew what God was up to.

That evening I asked the couple to meet me at my home and wrote them a one-thousand-dollar check. The man could not believe it. He looked at me and said that when I had told the story that morning prior to receiving the offering, he put his faith into action and gave a hundred-dollar bill that was to sustain them throughout the week. He was amazed at how God blessed his effort tenfold. I told him that was nothing compared to the fact that I had told God less than twelve hours before that I would like to be able to one day give a thousand dollars, and He not only provided the amount but told me who to give it to! How can I not expect God to do the unexpected when he shows up and shows out in such a fashion?

Jesus often did the unexpected. Nobody expected to get fed the day he took a few fish and some bread and threw a dinner for five thousand men plus women and children. I'm sure that Peter the fisherman was somewhat astounded when he found the money for his and Jesus' tax bill in the mouth of a wide mouth bass! Miracles are common, everyday occurrences for God. He dwells in the supernatural realm of heaven. His goal is to elevate our faith so that He can share His love with us. When you truly love someone, you want them to know you. You also want to be able to help them when they are in need. The more we open ourselves up to the possibility of the unexpected, the more we can expect to see God accomplish.

Expectant faith is undaunted by opposition. It is not hindered by natural odds that seem to be against us. I am reminded of how God brought the walls of Jericho down merely with a shout of victory from the children of Israel. I recall how God winnowed Gideon's army down from thirty-two thousand to three hundred and defeated the Midianites with nothing but a trumpet

EXPECTANT FAITH IS UNDAUNTED BY OPPOSITION.

and some lamps. I can't forget the story of Esther and how she trusted God to give her favor in a time and culture when women had no influence, and in turn saved an entire nation from genocide. God brought down a nine-foot giant with a small stone hurled by a small shepherd boy who was destined to be king. These are not fairy tales. These are building blocks meant to build expectant faith. God has not changed. Those people were no less flawed than we are. Our trials are not greater than theirs were. Everything God does is a miracle. We can expect the miraculous to occur if we trust the Lord!

CHAPTER 13

RESOLVE

Resolve that the answer will come,
but how it comes is God's business.

Nehemiah surveyed the work that had been accomplished thus far. It was only twenty-six days into a project that could have taken years. Yet, amazingly, they were almost halfway done. The walls of Jerusalem would be rebuilt, and the people could once again function with some level of peace and safety. Then opposition emerged from Sanballat, a regional governor under the king of Persia, and his allies. His name meant "strength," and it was his job to make the Jews feel hopeless and weak. He was an enemy of the Jews and didn't want them to have a place of protection and safety. He challenged them to battle on five occasions. When that did not slow progress, he joined with another regional governor named Tobiah to further hinder the project by threatening war. Tobiah mocked the work by saying that the wall would likely collapse under the weight of a small fox. Nevertheless, Jewish confederates of Sanballat in Jerusalem, attempts to intimidate, physical threats, discouragement, and political pressure did not deter Nehemiah.

Nehemiah likely reflected that not long before that, he was nothing more than a cupbearer for a heathen king. He poured wine into a cup and made sure that if arsenic was present, it would mean his own death and not the monarch's death. But due to a burden in his heart which resulted in a request to the king, he became the architect appointed to oversee one of the greatest projects in the history of Israel. He could not overlook God's hand in his life. He was aware of the enormity of the event. He understood that it was not going to be easy. He nevertheless resolved to see it through to the end. And see it through he did.

In exactly fifty-two days the walls and gates of Jerusalem were rebuilt, and the city was once again secure. It was not done with heavy equipment or massive machinery. It was accomplished with crude tools and willing hands. The people took ownership of the vision and had minds and hearts to work. Without Nehemiah's determination, it would have come to a screeching halt much to the delight of Sanballat and Tobiah. Nehemiah was determined to see the end of the story. He was not about to allow opposition to deter him from experiencing victory. He was resolved.

My dad grew up in the cotton fields of Texas and had some interesting words in his vocabulary. I often heard him use the word *stickability*. It's probably not in the dictionary, but the meaning is clear. It refers to what it takes for a person to "stick it out" and not give up. It is a way of describing the resolve to complete the task or see something through. Victorious faith requires resolve.

Resolve is not something that comes all by itself. It is usually facilitated by some of the traits we have already discussed. Patience provides the time needed for the resolve to develop and become established. Trust provides the peace of mind that resolve leans on when doubt tries to creep in. Maturity deters the inclination to give in to hasty action which undermines the master plan which only resolve can experience.

> RESOLVE IS THE BYPRODUCT OF COMPLETE FAITH AND THE FINAL TRAIT THAT IS NEEDED FOR VICTORIOUS OUTCOMES TO OUR TRIALS.

Joy continually refuels resolve any time the will to press on grows weak. Memory reminds us of the benefit of resolve as we recall the past battles won through determination and perseverance. In other words, resolve is the byproduct of complete faith and the final trait that is needed for victorious outcomes to our trials.

It was resolve that gave Daniel and his three Hebrew comrades the backbone to stand firm under the pressures of an ungodly king and a heathen culture. Sometimes, it takes resolve to do something that isn't popular. Other times resolve gives us the tenacity to not do something that everyone expects. In the case of these guys, both types can be seen. Shadrach, Meshach, and Abednego refused to

> RESOLVE WILL OFTEN HELP YOU CHOOSE THE PATH YOU NEED TO TAKE DESPITE THE DIFFICULTY THAT WAITS.

bow to a golden image when the entire province was on their knees. They were resolved to stay true to their convictions and God's Word even if it meant their death. Daniel went into his house and opened his windows towards Jerusalem and let his voice be heard when the edict had been given to pray to no other God, worshipping only King Nebuchadnezzar.

Resolve will often help you choose the path you need to take despite the difficulty that waits.

If the path was easy, there would be no need for resolve. There was a time in the Apostle Paul's life when everyone he ran across warned him of the impending doom that lay ahead for him. He kept walking forward. He knew that it was God's will for him to preach the Gospel to those in Rome and nothing was going to detour his progress. It cost him his life. Historians say that when he was beheaded, he literally ran to the chopping block. He knew he had been faithful, and his reward was waiting. He had resolved to finish his course.

Resolve will enable us to filter out the well-meaning advice of friends who do not understand the assurance of knowing you have received divine instruction. I recall when I determined to attend Bible college. I had been preaching for a while, but I knew in my heart that something was lacking. I knew I needed more knowledge and training.

> RESOLVE WILL ENABLE US TO FILTER OUT THE WELL-MEANING ADVICE OF FRIENDS WHO DO NOT UNDERSTAND THE ASSURANCE OF KNOWING YOU HAVE RECEIVED DIVINE INSTRUCTION.

I also knew I needed to grow beyond the boundaries that were established where I was currently. I would often pray that God would change me. One day He informed me that the kind of change I needed would not come without my involvement. It was not a gift He would bestow but rather a reward for my willingness to go through the process of change. Once I understood God's will, my path was established. My wife and I were resolved to fulfill that will.

As soon as our decision went public, things became challenging. Everyone from our parents to our pastors questioned our decision. We had decent jobs, and I had a wife and a little baby to take care of. I knew no one in Missouri, and no one knew me. We had just enough savings to move and pay the first installment on tuition. Worldly wisdom would be to rethink this crazy notion. However, we were resolved.

We struggled through four years with minimum wage jobs and less income than outgo. We faced opposition on several fronts. We never gave up. We were determined to see it through. It was the only way to discover what changes would await at the end of the process. We were not disappointed. I grew spiritually more than I ever would have otherwise. We were used in the ministry and learned more about faith than a seminary could ever teach a preacher in a hundred years. We saw miracles that only God could have performed. We discovered that God is faithful to those who show themselves to be faithful. Resolve had enabled us to reach a new level of faith that we would not have experienced had we remained in our safe zone.

Jesus was resolved to go all the way to the cross. He could have bailed if He had wanted. He could have said that we weren't worth it or that He was far too precious to be subjected to the humiliation and suffering He was to endure. His resolve could be summed up in one statement. "Not my will, but thine, be done" (Luke 22:42). He was determined to please the Father and do His will in spite

JESUS WAS RESOLVED TO GO ALL THE WAY TO THE CROSS.

of all that it entailed. It was not an easy choice as was witnessed by His struggle on the night of His betrayal. He sweated great drops of blood. He asked others to pray. He implored the Father to consider another means of salvation. But in the end, He was resolved.

We live in a world that is inundated with things that make life easy. We have everything from voice-controlled appliances to robotic vacuum cleaners. Our goal seems to be to accomplish as much as possible with as little effort as possible. That is not how God's economy works. There are times when God miraculously steps in and unloads the burden off our backs. Most often however there is a struggle involved that requires us to invest our time and effort. Our participation is driven by our resolve. Resolve encourages the spiritual disciplines we often lack otherwise.

RESOLVE ENCOURAGES THE SPIRITUAL DISCIPLINES WE OFTEN LACK OTHERWISE.

Prayer is a key factor in developing overcoming faith. Resolve is sustained by prayer. Trials often bring us to our knees. I read a story about a man that climbed a great mountain led by an experienced guide. As they reached the precipice the guide pulled his cohort to his knees. "You can't stand up here," he said. "The winds are so fierce they will blow you off the peak" he explained. Prayer is the only way we can withstand the winds of opposition that are always present anytime we are near the point of success. Believing that we can stand on our own strength is deadly. It requires the discipline of prayer. When we are determined to see the desired result of the trial, we will develop the resolve to pray. It is not an option. It is the lifeline that we must remain attached to lest we fall into the false mindset of self-sufficiency.

RESOLVE IS SUSTAINED BY PRAYER.

Prayer is the first thing that must be employed in the advent of a trial. I believe that one of the greatest lessons God uses trials to teach is that we need to develop and maintain the discipline of daily prayer. As a young believer, I struggled to make time for God every morning. The bed often felt so comfy, and the snooze button was so readily available. It was just too easy to deprive myself of the time I needed to spend with the Lord each day. I would excuse my lack of discipline by telling myself that I pray throughout the day or that God surely must be aware of my tiredness and knows I need the rest.

One day my wife posed a question to me. "If you knew that you had an appointment to meet with the President of the United States at five a.m., would you do what it takes to make that appointment?"

"Of course, I would," I replied.

"You have an appointment with the King of Kings tomorrow," she said. "Will you be there?"

I resolved that I was going to give God the first part of my day. I determined that I would develop the habit of meeting with God before I meet with anyone else each day. I learned that when I made God the first person on my list to talk with, it affected how I talked to everyone else that day.

I also resolved that my prayer would not be routine or ritualistic. Prayer that fails to touch heaven is not useless, but I have little use for it. I resolved that my prayer would not be concluded each day until I felt that I had been to the throne room of God. That may look or feel different for me than someone else. A person should be able to discern their connection to God through prayer regardless of their level of zeal or spiritual background. There are times when we don't feel spiritual. We often experience what many refer to as a season of dryness or a wilderness experience. I propose that there is no need for such a season. There is always an oasis in the middle of every spiritual desert. Jesus said that if we thirst, we need only come to Him. The resolve to pray all the way through the dry place to the point of refreshment is all that is required to put an end to dry seasons that too many embrace.

I find this strategy employed by every great man and woman of God. I have never met a spiritual giant that was not resolved to make prayer a priority. I strive to emulate them in hopes that I can tap into at least a portion of God's power and presence they experienced. When Joshua faced a city encompassed by great walls he prayed. He had no weaponry but prayer. When Hezekiah faced a terminal illness, he prayed. He knew that only God was the giver and taker of life. When Habakkuk saw unrighteousness everywhere and impending doom on the horizon of his nation, he prayed. He knew God had an unrevealed plan and he was right.

Prayer should be our knee-jerk reaction to a trial. It should not be our last resort. When I was in Bible college, I attended a church which had a youth pastor on staff.

PRAYER SHOULD BE OUR KNEE-JERK REACTION TO A TRIAL.

The job description of a youth pastor usually includes doing a lot of the work that no one else really wants to do. One day Randy came in from a hard day of mowing the college property and was ready to sit down to a hot meal his wife had prepared. Suddenly there was a knock at the door. He wondered to himself if he had left something undone, and if he would be allowed to enjoy his meal before it got cold.

He opened the door to find his next-door neighbor standing on his porch holding a lifeless baby in his arms. The baby was already blue, and it was obvious that it was not breathing. The neighbor was not a Christian, but he knew Randy was. He thrust the child in Randy's arms, and with tears in his eyes he pleaded, "Pray, Randy, pray." Randy did not have time to develop a prayer life or repent for some long-standing sin problem. Fortunately, before Randy headed out to mow the grass or change the oil in the church bus each morning, he afforded time in prayer with God. His resolve to be a man of prayer had prepared him for this moment of desperation. Randy prayed, and the child began breathing. By the time the 911 response team arrived there was no danger present. When we resolve ourselves to pray, we remain in a state of readiness.

We need to resolve to be people of praise. Satan hates praise probably more than prayer. After all, it was praise that resulted in the devil being banished from his place of prominence in heaven. He lusted after the glory that was being given to God. One of the things that causes Satan to be baffled more than anything else is the willingness of mere mortals to praise a God they have never seen. The angels have witnessed the glory of God. They have seen with their eyes the spectacular place we call heaven. They have experienced the fullness of God. We have not. Yet many of us have resolved that we are going to praise God with all that is in us. We don't do praise based on what we have seen. We praise by faith in what is proclaimed in His word and what He has done in our hearts. That infuriates the devil.

> SATAN HATES PRAISE PROBABLY MORE THAN PRAYER.

The resolve to praise despite hardship is like throwing gasoline on the fire of joy. As we have already discussed, the joy of the Lord is our strength. It takes resolve to praise God when things are not going well. It is a decision we make that is not overturned by opposition. It is not determined by our awareness of the situation we face. It is determined by awareness that God is God no matter what. He is still good and worthy of praise regardless of the circumstances. He deserves glory in the worst of situations. When we are in the middle of hardship, we need the resolve to live up to that expectation. Resolve affords us the strength to look at our child lying in a hospital bed and give God praise for His healing power. Resolve allows the ability to overlook the negative balance in our checkbook and praise God for His provisions. Resolve enables us to peer into a casket holding a spouse that was taken at a young age and praise God for His divine purpose. That is something neither the unbelieving world nor the enemy of our souls will ever understand.

> THE RESOLVE TO PRAISE DESPITE HARDSHIP IS LIKE THROWING GASOLINE ON THE FIRE OF JOY.

Victorious believers praise! Praise is an overflow of gratitude. The Bible tells us to give thanks in all situations. Our praise should not be selective. If there is a test, there is a reason for the test. Give thanks. Give thanks for all that has occurred thus far. Give thanks for what is currently being accomplished, and especially give thanks for what is about to happen. We can do so with certainty because we know who God is and that He loves us. Dr. Tony Evans once said that our attitude of gratitude will determine our altitude. The higher our level of praise, the closer to God we become.

My wife had a pastor as a little girl who had a brace on his leg due to a childhood disease. With each painful step he took, he offered God praise. Every step was accompanied by "thank you, Lord,"or "praise Jesus," or "I praise you, God" as well as many other expressions of gratitude. I did not personally know this man, but I can tell you something about him. He lived close to God and was able to face trials with confidence. I just imagine that Satan became anxious every morning when this man of God's feet hit the floor. We should resolve to be people of praise fueled by hearts of thanksgiving.

There is no means by which we can avoid trials. Trouble comes to all who live on this earth. The Bible declares that it rains on the just and the unjust (Matthew 5:45). We can only choose how we are going to navigate through those storms. We determine who is going to be at the helm. We must resolve that we will let Christ be the Captain of our ships. We are not equipped to sail through the troubled seas that threaten to capsize our lives. God does not expect us to have the ability to see ourselves safely to shore. He expects us to utilize the knowledge we have been given and to trust Him. We must resolve to relinquish the control of our lives to our Creator and Savior. That is the most important decision we can make.

John the Baptist said it best when he declared that "He must increase, but I must decrease" (John 3:30). The ultimate secret to victorious faith is total dependence on God. Allowing God to have control of our situations frees us from the anxiety that accompanies the uncertainty of the outcome. God never fails. He will always bring our trial to the desired end. I believe that if we allow God to be God and do what God does best, we can then focus on being who we need to be. Our job should be to develop and practice the traits of victorious faith. The result will be spiritual growth and victory.

These are truths that can't be learned with mere words on a page. The best teacher is experience. I pray that the messages I have shared in this book will be revisited time and again during the worst of trials. I hope that this book will be a survival guide of sorts that will aid the weary Christian traveler during the dark moments of their spiritual journey. I do not claim to have shared spiritual truths that have yet to be discovered. I only seek to remind us of the truths that have always existed. I desire to refocus our attention from the challenge we face to the means by which so many before us have emerged as champions.

Finally, I must remind us that we do not go through any trial unnoticed. Someone close to us is always observing how we face our struggles. We are always in the process

OUR SPIRITUAL FOOTPRINTS MUST BE DEEP AND WELL PLANTED.

of leaving a legacy. Others will find guidance and direction by our actions much like spiritual bread crumbs that fall on the path we travel. Our children and grandchildren are forming opinions based on how well we put our words into action. They must be shown the way. How can we leave the markers they need to navigate life if we are unable or unwilling to lead by example? Our spiritual footprints must be deep and well planted.

I grew up in Dallas, Texas the home of the State Fair of Texas. I went numerous times as a child and as an adult. I formed some great memories there but none as lasting as the time my dad took my older brother and me. It was 1962, and I was five years old. My dad had a talk with my brother and me just before entering the fairground gates. He informed us that he had just enough funds to get us into the fair and to buy a few corn dogs. He made sure we understood that we would not be able to enjoy any rides or special attractions. It was all he could do to just get us there.

We walked around the grounds most of the day taking in the exhibits and checking out the latest models of automobiles and appliances, as well as the various forms of livestock. Finally, it was time to go home. From where we were standing, we could see the Midway where all the carnies were barking out their appeal to play their games as well as the many rides and attractions. We convinced Dad to walk us down the Midway and back so long as we promised not to ask to stop along the way.

The place was crowded more than anywhere I had ever been. It was literally like cattle pressed up against one another seeming to move in concert slowly down the wide stretch of asphalt. I held tight to my father's hand. I was enthralled with all the sights and sounds and smells. Suddenly fear gripped my heart. My dad had let go of my hand. I quickly looked over just in time to see him bend down and pick up a twenty-dollar bill. Twenty dollars was a lot of money in 1962, and those rides cost little more than a quarter admission. My brother's eyes met mine and no words needed spoken. We smiled thinking to ourselves what a tremendous stroke of luck this was and imagining how much fun we were about to have.

That's when our dad did something inconceivable to most. He looked at that bill and then he looked at his sons. He slowly turned around and led us to the Lost and Found department at the State Fair of Texas. Thousands of people had entered those gates that day, and the thought that any lost funds could possibly be recouped by the owner would have been unthinkable to any rational person. In addition, I have no doubt that there were probably numerous practical needs that we had that could have been met with the newfound treasure as well. None of that took precedence over the opportunity for my dad to exhibit to his children what honest, ethical character looked like in action. The overweight fair employee looked shocked and dismayed. He stuffed the bill in his pocket as we walked out of his office.

We could have had the time of our lives that day, and I would likely have never forgotten it, but I would not be writing about it. A good time rarely changes your life or impacts you in a way that is irreversible. My dad saw an opportunity to teach a life lesson and implant within us the importance of faith and obedience. He was a man of God. He was not going to act in a way that would make us doubt the reality of his relationship with Christ. He would not sell out his character for twenty dollars. And my brother and I were watching. My brother and I spoke of this event numerous times and did so with respect and honor for our dad.

YOU ARE A SERMON BEING PREACHED ON THE OVERCOMING FAITH THAT CHRIST BOUGHT AND PAID FOR. YOUR ACTIONS AND ATTITUDES ARE THE WORDS ON THE PAGE THAT OTHERS ARE READING AND LEARNING FROM.

The trial you are going through is being observed by someone. You are not going through a process which only affects yourself. You are a sermon being preached on the overcoming faith that Christ bought and paid for. Your actions and attitudes are the words on the page that others are reading and learning from.

> LET IT BE SAID THAT VICTORIOUS FAITH CAN BE HAD BY ANYONE WHO SEEKS IT. LET IT BE SAID THAT I WAS RESOLVED TO SEE IT THROUGH.

When I am gone, I want some things to be able to be said about me. Let it be said that I was a very flawed person who was desperately in need of a Savior each and every day. Let it be said that only by the grace of God was I able to find acceptance in the eyes of a holy God. Let it be said that God never failed to meet my needs. Let it be said that I was an overcomer. Let it be said that victorious faith can be had by anyone who seeks it. Let it be said that I was resolved to see it through.

The End

To contact Gary for a speaking engagement
or to stay up to date on upcoming books,
visit his website at: **Garymduke.com**

Note from the Publisher

Are you a first time author?

Not sure how to proceed to get your book published?
Want to keep all your rights and all your royalties?
Want it to look as good as a Top 10 publisher?
Need help with editing, layout, cover design?
Want it out there selling in 90 days or less?

Visit our website for some exciting new options!

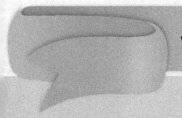

www.chalfant-eckert-publishing.com

CPSIA information can be obtained
at www.ICGtesting.com
Printed in the USA
LVHW081446240319
611642LV00039B/1978/P